A
Twaddle-Free
Education

An Introduction to Charlotte Mason's Timeless Educational Ideas

DEBORAH TAYLOR-HOUGH

ISBN-13: 978-0692431283
ISBN-10: 0692431284

DEDICATION

To dedicated parent-teachers everywhere.

CONTENTS

INTRODUCTION

As a long-time home educator——all three of my adult children were homeschooled from preschool through high school graduation——I've become convinced that education is so much more than a just scope-and-sequence, or a series of facts to learn, or a particular set of books, or passing standardized tests. I wanted my children to leave their homeschooling years with a lifetime love of learning. I didn't want their education to work like an inoculation, giving them just enough education to make them immune to it for the rest of their lives.

I wanted to instill a hunger and thirst for great books, fine art, natural sciences, theology, philosophy, and everything else our world has to offer. I personally am convinced that Charlotte Mason's methods and ideas are the best way to accomplish this lofty goal.

Mason developed a lifetime love of learning in her students by engaging the children firsthand with nature, literature, science, history, art, music, and avoiding dumbed-down materials as much as possible. The main focus of Mason's educational ideas and philosophy was having the students read top quality literature——real books rather than textbooks——and delving into a wide variety of serious topics throughout childhood. Mason described most literature written to children as "twaddle" and felt that childish materials should be avoided at all costs. And this was one hundred years ago. Dumbed-down, childish materials aren't something new. Keep in mind that just because something was published a long time ago, it isn't necessarily great literature.

Believing that Mason's teachings are timeless, I'm not afraid to move those ideas out of the past into the modern age. While I enjoy Victorian decor as much as the next person, I believe Charlotte Mason would've made use of every modern convenience, new development, and scientific method available. She was considered a bit avant-garde in her day … and I believe she surely would've been considered cutting-edge if she lived today, as well.

This book isn't a how-to or a complete overview of everything Charlotte Mason-related. It's just one mom's experiences with applying these methods for many years in an American homeschool setting. If this book simply leads someone else to investigate Charlotte Mason's ideas further for their own homeschooling adventures, I'll feel my purpose in putting these writings together was well served.

Happy homeschooling to you and yours!

Deborah Taylor-Hough
Seattle/Tacoma 2015

1

WHO IS CHARLOTTE MASON?

Charlotte Mason was a British educator from the early part of the 20th Century. Her methods and philosophies have recently experienced a resurgence—especially among American homeschooling families. Her emphasis on developing a lifetime love of learning was in stark contrast to the almost anti-child climate of her time. According to a World Wide Education Service (WES), pamphlet Charlotte Mason lived in an era when …

> "…they practised reading, writing and arithmetic, sitting bolt upright on hard chairs (no slouching was allowed!) and writing on a piece of slate which could be wiped clean and used again. They were often given long lists to learn by heart, such as capital cities or dates

from history or hard spellings. If they did not learn their work they were punished, sometimes by caning…"

In response to her own experiences and education, Mason conducted lectures, wrote numerous books on educational topics, founded a school for training governesses and others working with children in her methods, and published a monthly periodical called The Parents' Review which allowed her to stay in touch with her followers throughout the world. Mason's philosophies were originally used by governesses in England to educate (i.e.: homeschool) the children in their charge. Eventually the Parents' Union Schools based on her philosophies sprung up throughout England, and her training school became a college to supply teachers for the Parents' Union Schools.

Charlotte Mason had a deep love of children and a concern that they develop a lifetime love of learning. Her method provides for a generous Liberal Arts interdisciplinary education. Her method is based on core subjects and incorporates the fine arts.

A primary emphasis of Mason's educational philosophy was having the students read top quality literature—real books rather than textbooks—and delving into a wide variety of serious topics throughout childhood. Mason described most literature written to children as "twaddle" and felt that childish materials should be avoided at all costs.

Charlotte Mason is sometimes referred to as the founder of the modern homeschooling movement, although her name was virtually unknown to American homeschoolers for many years. Mason's original writings were rediscovered by Susan Schaeffer-Macaulay (author of *For the Children's Sake*) in the late 1970's and eventually brought back into print by Karen Andreola (original publisher of *The Original Homeschooling Series* and author of *A Charlotte Mason Companion*).

Charlotte Mason's original six-volume set can be borrowed from your local library through interlibrary loan, purchased online, and is also available digitally for free on several websites including:

- AmblesideOnline.org
- AmblesideSchools.com

2

MY INTRODUCTION TO CHARLOTTE MASON

As time goes by, I've come to appreciate the numerous methods Charlotte Mason used with her students. But when I first became acquainted with the name Charlotte Mason, I really wasn't aware of many of the details.

I was initially drawn to Charlotte Mason's ideas after reading Susan Schaeffer-Macaulay's book, *For the Children's Sake: Foundations of Education for Home and School* (FTCS). This gentle, insightful book opened my eyes to the joy that I could find within our family and our homeschooling endeavors. I've read and re-read FTCS a number of times, and with each reading I find it refreshes my soul and restores my vision for what homeschooling can be about. I was already committed to home education when I first read FTCS, but the book helped cement my dreams and visions for our family. It also gave me reassurance that I, as my children's mother, could provide not just an adequate education, but a rich and full educational experience for my children.

I remembered all too well the long hours spent idly during my own childhood sitting in school reading dry-as-dust textbooks, studying only to pass the test, learning to play the "game" of pleasing the teacher, and always feeling that there was so much more out there in life to learn about, ponder and experience.

I wanted so much more for my own children. I wanted them to feast their hearts, souls and minds on fine literature, awe-inspiring art, majestic music, and great thoughts. I wanted them to learn how to think— not just learn to pass a test. I wanted them to be prepared intellectually, spiritually, morally and academically to pursue wholeheartedly whatever passion was on their hearts for the future, whatever those passions might be, whether in the field of medicine, art, education, missions, or homemaking.

Children are Born Persons

Charlotte Mason believed that children are born persons. They are not possessions, nor cogs in the machine, nor simply warm bodies to feed and clothe. From the very beginning, children are individuals with a spark of life all their own—their own dreams, desires, spiritual hungers, and giftings. Children have capable minds which need to be respected, not devalued with "twaddle" or dumbed down literature.

I remember as a child being frustrated by Sesame Street when it first came on the air back in the sixties. I was only about seven or eight at the time, but I remember sitting in front of the television with my two younger next-door neighbors and feeling horrified by the twaddle being paraded in front of my eyes. Why should I watch something ridiculous like that when I could curl up with Beatrix Potter or any number of favorite authors and have my imagination encouraged and my heart enlarged? The quality and content of Sesame Street changed and developed over the years, but when the series first began, it was empty and consisted of nothing more than the most rudimentary educational twaddle.

The Importance of Play

Play is an important—no, an essential—part of childhood. Macaulay states in FTCS that "one of the saddest things I know is to watch students at L'Abri look at a group of children, involved for hours in satisfying play, and comment, 'I've never seen children playing like that.' No? Then weep. Even childhood is robbed of the richness of humanity."

Now-a-days, the myriads of organized sports and outside activities children participate in from preschool on up, seem to be almost the antithesis of that healthy, hearty, spontaneous, and child-directed play which goes into shaping the character, dreams, and thoughts of an individual growing person.

I remember the long afternoon hours of play on our street where I grew up. Mud pies were the feast of the day, impromptu races of various sorts kept us active and healthy, relaxed ball games that included everyone (even the youngest or least coordinated of the children), building forts, driving our "motorcycles" (ie: tricycles), and even acting out our own made-up scenes from Gilligan's Island with all the neighborhood children playing their favorite characters. I know I could argue that watching Gilligan's Island in the first place was a rather non-educational event, but the natural play that occurred as we acted out our respective roles was important. I always wanted to play the Professor. He was one of my childhood heroes. Any man who could make a radio out of coconuts and spend his day surrounded by test tubes and beakers, never losing his logical take on life, was someone after my own heart. I was a rather odd kid! Odd, maybe. But I was me—totally individual in my thinking and make up. And I think that takes us back to the idea of children being born persons. Fortunately, no one came and interrupted our well-developed game and said that I couldn't play the Professor because I was a girl. I was allowed to give free reign to my imagination and fully explore, through the simple joys of play, what I thought it would mean to be a scientist as an adult.

Maybe playing Gilligan's Island seems a bit silly, but we played with all our hearts and it was a game totally of our own devising, no adults telling us what to do or how to do it. By the way, as an adult I did end up working in a medical laboratory—surrounded by test tubes and beakers.

Living Books

One of the most valuable activities in our home is reading often and at length from good books, "living" books, chosen carefully for their literary value— interesting, educational and pleasurable to read. I remember my grandmother baby-sitting me often when I was quite young. Each night she'd read one of the Beatrix Potter books to me. Those moments curled up, warm under the covers with Grandma sitting on a chair beside the guest bed reading delightful stories about Peter Rabbit, Tom Kitten, and Benjamin Bunny are some of my warmest and fondest childhood memories. As an adult, reading those same books to my own children evoked happiness in the deepest part of my being.

I started reading aloud to my children when they were just days old. They couldn't understand the content of the reading yet, but I knew that the love and care communicated to them by being held in my arms as I read softly to them was a gift beyond measure. By the time my children were about three-years-old, they were all able to sit and listen to chapter books. Books like *Charlotte's Web* or *Winnie-the-Pooh*. Not dumbed-down condensed or abridged versions of the Pooh books, by the way, but the original A .A. Milne classics.

Once my children were reading fluently on their own, they did their school work from their own books, but we still continued our family read aloud times just for the fun of it. I kept reading aloud to my children for as long as they were living in my home. Reading aloud with children can become almost an obsession once you experience the joy and wonder it brings.

I think all the reading aloud in our home did wonders for our family. It served as a treasured family activity, a foundation for a love a great literature in the children, a means for developing a stronger command of the language, and an avenue for increasing listening skills.

Narration

Charlotte Mason's idea of having children narrate what they're learning resonated deeply with me. Narration is essentially just retelling what you've heard, seen, or experienced—thus cementing the learning process.

The whole idea of narration made sense because I saw how natural it was to want to tell someone about a good book or a fun movie, and then in the retelling, the story seemed to come alive all over again, living in the memory in a new way because of the retelling. I also saw clearly that if someone knew they would have to retell something they had read or seen, they would listen more intently.

That's pretty much the in-a-nutshell version of what first drew me to many of Charlotte Mason's methods and philosophies. But the more I learned about her methods and the more of her ideas I applied with my own children, the more convinced I became that these ideas were the right method for our family.

The application and adaptations of Mason's methods described here and later in this book are solely mine. I honestly don't claim to speak for Charlotte Mason. One thing I've discovered with homeschoolers in general is we tend to be a pretty independent-minded group. Since each family is made up of a collection of unique individuals, it makes sense that my applications of these ideas in our home would be different from someone else's applications.

As Catherine Levison, author of *A Charlotte Mason Education*, humorously states in her seminars, the Charlotte Mason "police" won't be showing up on anyone's doorstep. I always felt the freedom to educate my children with the combination of methods and philosophies that we thoughtfully and prayerfully decided were best for our home.

I want to be sure to give Charlotte Mason full credit for being such a great inspiration to me. Our family's home education efforts have been greatly enhanced by the methods and ideas revealed through Charlotte Mason's writings.

3

CHARLOTTE MASON IN A NUTSHELL

Charlotte Mason was a big thinker who had a very high view of children. So let me start out by saying that I don't believe anyone could ever fit Charlotte Mason's ideas, methods, and philosophies into an actual nutshell. I just thought it made a good title for this overview.

Mason's ideas were so broad and far reaching, it took six large volumes to contain her writings on just the topic of education. With that said, here's a very brief overview of a handful of Charlotte Mason's most familiar ideas.

1) Avoid Twaddle in Reading Materials

Twaddle is what parents and educators today might call "dumbed down" literature. It is serving your children intellectual happy meals, rather than healthy, substantive mind- and soul-building foods. Charlotte Mason advocated avoiding twaddle and feasting children's hearts and minds on the best literary works available.

2) Read Living Books and Whole Books

Living books are the opposite of dull, dry textbooks. The people, places and events come alive as you read a living book. The stories touch your mind and heart. They are timeless. Whole books are the entirety of what the author actually wrote. If the author wrote a book, read the whole book. The opposite of this would be anthologies that include only snippets from other works—maybe a chapter from Dickens, a couple of paragraphs from Tolstoy, etc.

3) Practice Narration Rather than Taking Tests

Narration is the process of telling back what has been learned or read. Narrations are usually done orally, but as the child grows older (around age 12) and his writing skills increase, the narrations can be written, as well. Narration can also be accomplished creatively: painting, drawing, sculpting, play-acting, etc.

4)   Use Short Lessons

Charlotte Mason recommended spending short, focused periods of time on a wide variety of subjects. Lessons in the early years are only 10-15 minutes in length, but get progressively longer as the children mature. Lessons increase closer to an hour per subject for high school students.

Charlotte Mason says, this "idea of definite work to be finished in a given time is valuable to the child, not only as training him in habits of order, but in diligence; he learns that one time is not 'as good as another'; that there is no right time left for what is not done in its own time; and this knowledge alone does a great deal to secure the child's attention to his work. Again, the lessons are short, seldom more than twenty minutes in length for children under eight; and this, for two or three reasons. The sense that there is not much time for his sums or his reading, keeps the child's wits on the alert and helps to fix his attention; he has time to learn just so much of any one object as it is good for him to take in at once: and if the lessons be judiciously alternated—sums first, say, while the brain is quite fresh; then writing, or reading—some more or less mechanical exercise, by way of a rest; and so on, the program varying a little from day to day, but the same principle throughout—a 'thinking' lesson first, and a 'painstaking' lesson to follow,—the child gets through his morning lessons without any sign of weariness."

5) Take Weekly Nature Walks

In spite of often rainy, inclement weather, Charlotte Mason insisted on going out once-a-week for an official Nature Walk, allowing the children to experience and observe the natural environment firsthand. These excursions should be nature walks, not nature talks.

6) Keep Nature Notebooks

Nature Notebooks are artist sketchbooks containing pictures the children have personally drawn of plants, wildlife or any other natural object found in its natural setting. These nature journals can also include nature-related poetry, prose, detailed descriptions, weather notes, Latin names, etc.

7) Take Daily Walks

In addition to the weekly Nature Walks, Mason also recommended children spend large quantities of time outside each day, no matter what the weather. Take a daily walk for fun and fresh air.

8) Include Art Appreciation through Picture Study

Bring the child into direct contact with the best art. Choose one artist at a time; six paintings per artist; study one painting per week (maybe 15 minutes per week). Allow the child to look at the work of art intently for a period of time (maybe five minutes). Have him take in every detail. Then take the picture away and have him narrate (tell back) what he's seen in the picture.

9) Practice Journaling

There's great value in keeping a personal journal, encouraging reflection and descriptive writing. Record activities, thoughts and feelings, favorite sayings, personal mottoes, favorite poems, etc.

10) Use Copywork and Dictation

Daily copywork provides on-going practice for handwriting, spelling, grammar, etc. Keep a notebook handy that's specifically for copying noteworthy poems, prose, quotes, etc. Each day choose a paragraph, or sentence, or page (depending on the age of child). Have the child practice writing it perfectly during his copywork time. Have them look carefully at all punctuation, capital letters, etc. When the child knows the passage well, dictate the passage to the child for him to recreate the passage.

11) Keep a Book of the Centuries

A Book of the Centuries is a glorified homemade timeline; usually a notebook containing one or two pages per century. As children learn historical facts, they make notes in their book on the appropriate century's page about famous people, important events, inventions, wars, battles, etc.

12) Use the Afternoon for Free-time and Handicrafts

Charlotte Mason's schools finished daily academics in the morning, allowing the afternoon hours for free time to pursue crafts and other leisure activities or areas of personal interest.

13) Establish Good Habits

Charlotte Mason had much to say on establishing good habits in children. Habits (good or bad) are like the ruts in a path from a wheelbarrow going down the same trail again and again. As time goes on, it becomes increasingly difficult to run the wheelbarrow outside the rut, but the wheel will always run smoothly down the well-worn rut in the path.

By training children in good habits, the school day (and home life in general) goes more smoothly. Focus on one habit at a time for 4-6 weeks rather than attempting to implement a long list of new habits all at once.

Where to Begin

If you've only just recently been introduced to Charlotte Mason's ideas but have already purchased this year's books or curriculum, don't worry. You don't have to throw out your entire curriculum or all of those expensive textbooks (at least not yet). Just try adding one or two new ideas or methods at a time. Work on building these ideas into your home school as new habits over the course of the year.

Narration
- Do oral narrations only to begin with (written narrations come much later and never completely replace oral narration)
- No corrections / no questions

Book Choice
- Living books
- Twaddle-free (not dumbed-down for kids)
- Read aloud
- Whole books (the entirety of what the author

wrote)

Nature Study
- Nature walks (*not* nature talks)
- Nature notebooks
- Leaf collections
- Bird watching
- Bird feeder
- Bird book

Short Lessons
- Ten minutes to fifteen minutes per subject
- Alternate subject matter—heavy vs. light topics or mental vs. physical effort

Free-time in the afternoons
- Finish academics before lunch
- Work on arts and crafts
- Go outside for a walk, or as Charlotte Mason might say, "have a scamper on the lawn"

I also recommend before giving too many assignments to your child, start out by giving yourself the following reading and narration assignment. In addition to the book you're currently holding in your hand, read at least one of the following titles:

- *For the Children's Sake* by Susan Schaeffer Macaulay
- *A Charlotte Mason Education* by Catherine Levison
- *Charlotte Mason Companion* by Karen Andreola
- *Home Education* by Charlotte Mason
- *Charlotte Mason Summaries* by Leslie Noelani Laurio

As you read, write out a one or two paragraph narration after each chapter. Don't look at your notes or flip back through the book while writing. Just tell what you remember. Or narrate orally what you've been reading to your spouse, to a friend, or to an older child/student.

4

THE FORMATION OF HABITS

I've been a long-time fan of Charlotte Mason's educational ideas, but my favorite idea of hers doesn't even apply strictly to education. It's the whole concept of developing habits into the life of a child as they grow.

Charlotte Mason had much to say on establishing good habits in children. Habits (good or bad) are like the ruts in a path from a wheelbarrow going down the same trail again and again. As time goes on, it becomes increasingly difficult to run the wheelbarrow outside the rut, but the wheel will always run smoothly down the well-worn rut in the path. By training children in good habits, the school day (and home life in general) goes more smoothly. Focus on one habit at a time for 4-6 weeks rather than attempting to implement a long list of new habits all at once.

The habit formation pages of my personal copy of Charlotte Mason's book, *Home Education*, are nearly dog-eared from consistently referring back to them for inspiration and reference, so I decided to put together a small volume with the pertinent information all in one place for my own use. Much to my surprise, I've heard from other people that they'd been desiring a similar smaller book just focusing on Miss Mason's habit formation teaching, and so the small book, *Habits: The Mother's Secret of Success*, was born. It's essentially a compilation of Charlotte Mason's writings on the topic of habit formation. You can order the *Habits* book online from Amazon. *Habits* is the first volume in the Charlotte Mason Topics series.

I hope it inspires you to read more of Charlotte Mason's work for yourself and discover the wealth of ideas her writing continues to impart to modern day parents, educators, and homeschoolers throughout the world.

One Habit at a Time

Not only is habit building a great tool for child-training, it's also an excellent way to implement new growth into your own life, as well. I've been told it takes four to six weeks for any action to become a habit. So, keeping that in mind, one way I'm going to insure my success at keeping my New Year's resolutions this next year is by working on only one new habit at a time each month. Then every time I turn to a new calendar page, I'll work on developing a different good habit. At the end of the year, I could easily have twelve new positive habits in my life. Once something's become a habit, it's simply a part of my life and not something I'll even have to think about anymore.

Here are some sample goals and habits I planned one year a long time ago to implement in no particular order. I took these things one at time, and only one per month.

- Use both an aerobic video and my exercise equipment 3-4 times per week
- Spend 20-30 minutes reading aloud to my children everyday
- Get up at 5am for personal prayer, and Bible study
- Work on my next book for half an hour everyday
- Spend ten minutes each day decluttering

If I had started the New Year off by attempting to do each one of these things at the same time, I knew I would quickly become overwhelmed, and give up long before any of these activities became habitual and second-nature. What's the area of life you're most concerned about? Exercise? Weight loss? Healthy eating? Getting organized? Saving money? Spending more time with your kids? Break your goal down into simple steps that you can easily manage, and then start working your way to your goal, one small step at a time. As the old cliche' says: How do you eat an elephant? One bite at a time.

By making small and consistent changes, it's possible to change your health, your body, and your life. And the life and education of your children, too.

5

POETRY MEMORIZATION

Poetry memorization is a fun activity for kids and adults alike. What I've done with poems that we were going to learn is this: I would put the poem into my word processing program, and then I'd increase the font size so that the poem took up one entire typewritten page. Then I printed it out, slid the printed sheet into a plastic page protector, and hung it in a highly visible place in the house where the kids would see it regularly (i.e.: on the refrigerator, the classroom wall, or even in the bathroom!).

Several times each day, we would stop by the displayed poem and read it aloud together. After we were done memorizing a poem, I'd place the poem and its plastic page protector into a three-ring binder to use with subsequent children.

It's amazing how quickly you and your children will have an entire poem memorized with very little effort.

And with seasonal poems, you could recite at a family gathering such as an upcoming Easter or Thanksgiving dinner. You can impress Grandma—and make poetry memorization and recitation into a fun-filled family event.

6

WHO'S AFRAID OF THE BIG, BAD BARD?

Many years ago, we added Shakespeare to our family's educational activities for the first time. My oldest daughter loved our field trip to the Oregon Shakespeare Festival in Ashland, and I don't think I ever would have thought of introducing my children to The Bard at such a young age if it weren't for the inspiration of Charlotte Mason and some of the people writing on Charlotte Mason topics at the time such as Catherine Levison and Karen Andreola.

Before we chose a play to study, we looked at the schedule for the Oregon Shakespeare Festival. We decided the most child-friendly plays that season were A Midsummer Night's Dream and A Comedy of Errors. Since we were able to prepare more fully for seeing Dream, I'll tell you what we did in preparation for that particular play.

First, we read through Charles and Mary Lamb's version of "A Midsummer Night's Dream" in *Tales from Shakespeare* just to enjoy the plot and make sure we understood the basic story line before attempting to wade through the Elizabethan English of the play, itself.

Then we read Dream aloud together. It was amazing how quickly we began reading the original work with ease. The first scene or two was a struggle for me to read aloud since I hadn't had much personal experience with Shakespeare other than a class in high school and seeing several plays. But before long, I found myself not only reading the language fluently, but also starting to think in Shakespearean-type phrases. It really grows on you!

After we read through the play itself (twice), we went to the local library's inter-library loan system and checked out a video of the New York Shakespeare Festival's production of Dream. Seeing William Hurt as Oberon, King of the Fairies was interesting—a very unusual rendering of the part. We watched the video several times, and even my eight-year-old son enjoyed it tremendously.

Then for the grand finale of our study, my daughter and I saw A Midsummer Night's Dream performed live during our trip to Ashland. It was all-in-all a wonderful experience.

When preparing for A Comedy of Errors, we weren't able to locate a video tape of the play, and the audio tape we found wasn't very high quality, so we sufficed with reading the play itself several times and then seeing it performed live.

Personally, there's nothing quite like seeing a live production of Shakespeare. His plays were intended to be seen performed on the stage with live actors—not just read from a book with all the stage directions, etc.

If you don't have a professional Shakespearean company close by, don't despair. Check for local high school and college productions of Shakespeare's plays (these are often very good productions and not nearly as expensive as seeing a professional Shakespearean company).

Also, I regularly check through our local "What's Happening" guide in the newspaper and frequently find Shakespeare being offered in nearby towns and with local production companies.

7

NARRATION TIPS

Since people frequently ask me how to deal with multiple children narrating when reading to the kids all together, I'll give a brief answer about how we've dealt with this issue in our home.

After each reading selection, I would call on one of the children to narrate—they wouldn't know who it would be from one time to the next. Sometimes if I felt the first narration was sketchy, I'd call on one of the others to narrate any additional information he or she wanted to add.

We did brief oral narrations after every subject each day—whether the subject was covered together orally or studied independently. We only did written narrations a couple of times a week (at most) for a few carefully chosen subjects.

Many times people starting narration for the first time discover that their children are hesitant to narrate.

When asked to tell about the story, the child responds, "I don't know" or "I don't remember."

If you're hearing "I don't know" constantly, one of several things could be happening. Perhaps the material is too difficult for the child, or the passage could be too long. For beginners, have them do a narration after reading only a short paragraph or two. Possibly the child just isn't experienced enough with narration yet to attempt anything long or complex.

When we were first starting to use oral narrations, I found that *Aesop's Fables* and Beatrix Potter's books contained just about the right amount of material for my beginning narrators. These books contained short stories that could be read completely in one easy sitting.

One trick I learned to help the reluctant narrator is this: when I would hear the "I don't know/I don't remember" response, I would say something goofy that absolutely nothing to do with the story in question (with a smiling glint in my eye), such as: "So, the little red wagon turned into a purple frog. Is that what happened?"

Then my reluctant little narrator would laugh and say, "No, Mommy! That's not what happened—you're so funny!"

And then with a giggle and a huge smile, they would be off and running, giving me a detailed description of the very same story they "didn't remember" moments before.

Works every time.

8

NATURAL NATURE LEARNING

Our family hasn't been blessed with acres of property off in the country for our children to frolic to their hearts content. But a small city lot and many local parks have offered us tremendous opportunities for outdoor learning activities.

Parks

To make up for the lack of open natural space in our neighborhood, we go to various local parks at least two to three times per week. We don't go to the parks for the play equipment but for the exposure to a more natural setting. We are about half-an-hour driving time from Puget Sound so we often frequent parks with direct beach access.

When the tide's out, the kids explore tide pools, find crabs and enjoy the fresh salt air. Digging in the sand and making castles and roadways is always fun, too!

There's a "wilderness" park in our town which has access to a river bank, several walking trails through undisturbed woods, and a big open field for frolic and running.

Observations

One year, we started bringing the children's Nature Notebooks whenever we went to the wilderness park. Nature Notebooks are artist sketchbooks where the children can draw whatever natural items strike their fancy.

Throughout the fall, we revisited the wilderness park once each week and kept track of the changes we observed as the season progressed. Everything was green and full of leaves, at first. Then we saw the gradual change of colors, until finally, after an early snow storm, the trees were bare and the ground covered with leaves.

We casually discussed the difference between deciduous and evergreen trees and the kids really saw first-hand what that means. At first, the evergreens were barely visible amongst the heavy foliage. After the autumn leaves were gone, the evergreens were the only observable green in the woods.

The kids also noticed on their own that the level of the river had gradually gone down over the several months we'd been observing it.

We watched a large group of mushrooms spring up and practically overrun a section of the park's grass. The kids had great fun sketching the odd-looking mushrooms with their funny little caps. "They're like little umbrellas, Mom!"

One day, my oldest daughter sat entranced by a Black-Capped Chickadee darting between the branches of an autumn-clad maple. Although she had her Nature Notebook with her, the busy little bird just wasn't cooperating and holding still for his portrait.

When we arrived home, my daughter ran to the bookcase and grabbed a bird identification book. After looking up Chickadees, she used the illustration in the book as the model for the sketch she then added to her Nature Notebook. She also drew in a background of various trees we had seen at the park.

Backyard Bird Survey

Another simple Nature activity we've participated in right in our own small yard is the Backyard Bird Survey sponsored by the Washington State Department of Fish and Wildlife. I know that many other States offer similar programs, so if you're interested, contact your local Department of Fish and Wildlife to find out more.

The way the Backyard Bird Survey works: we do a bird count in our yard for a two hour stretch of time twice during each two week observation period. This surveying goes on throughout the winter months.

By participating in the Survey, we've learned a great deal about bird identification and the children have actually started bird watching at other times and in other places as well. The binoculars have become a favorite "toy."

One time during our Survey hours, we saw a Sharp-Shinned Hawk snatch a small House Finch off our feeder. Rather traumatic—especially since the hawk ate its meal in an open tree within our line of sight—but a much better learning experience than the best wildlife drama on television!

Encouragement

I want to encourage those of you who might not have easy access to your own fields and forests, there are other readily available opportunities for outdoor play and learning activities.

I can't stress enough how valuable I've found the Nature Notebook idea to be. We tried to remember to take our Nature Notebooks (I keep one too) with us whenever we'd go on any sort of outdoor adventure. Even trips to the local zoo could probably benefit from their own sketchbook. My understanding of the Nature Notebook idea, however, is that it should only contain sketches of objects the child has actually seen first-hand in natural settings. Perhaps zoo trips would require a separate Zoo Notebook.

9

NATURE NOTEBOOKS

Nature Notebooks are artist sketchbooks where the children can draw whatever natural items strike their fancy. The more options you offer the child, the more likely they'll find one or more ideas that spark their interest.

Entries in a Nature Notebook should be voluntary, by the way—not an assignment or a plea from the parent ("Now, draw the pretty bird for Mommy, honey. . . .").

- Information from first-hand observation the child has done themselves (not things they've learned from "teaching" or in the classroom).

- Drawings of leaves, flowers, birds, insects or anything else discovered by the child in its natural setting.

- Labels for their drawings—both English and Latin names if applicable.

- Notations on where the object was found.

- Notations about the temperature or weather conditions, dates, etc.

- Life cycles of plants. Draw the bare tree in winter; the spring buds; the summer blooms; the fall colors and seed pods. Or in a backyard garden you could draw a seed; draw the sprouting seedling; draw the full grown plant; draw the stem, leaves, flower, etc.; draw the fruit, vegetable or flower; draw the new seeds for starting the cycle again.

- Draw and describe an ant hill or a bee's nest.

- Take out a hand-held high-power magnifying glass and draw the intricate details of a bee's wing, or whatever else might be fascinating viewed through a magnifying lens.

- Pressing and mounting leaves or dried flowers.

- Samples of different types of leaves: divided, heart-shaped, fluted, needles, etc.

- Samples or drawings of different types of seeds: nuts; seed pods; seeds that fall to the ground; seeds that float through the air; etc.

- Parts of the flower: petal, sepal, stamen, etc.

- Sketches of animal tracks.

- Sketches of the life cycles of animals. Caterpillar to cocoon (or chrysalis) to moth (or butterfly); or egg to tadpole to frog (or salamander).

- Nature-related poems or quotes. The poems can be ones found during the child's reading time, or poems composed by the child.

For an outstanding example of a fully developed Nature Diary, take a look at the beautiful book *The Country Diary of an Edwardian Lady, 1906*. This book is currently out-of-print, but you can have Amazon.com do an out-of-print book search for you.

I also highly recommend the book, *Keeping a Nature Journal: Discovering a Whole New Way of Seeing the World Around You*, by Clare Walker Leslie and Charles E. Roth. The book is written and illustrated by science educators who use Nature Journals as their primary way of teaching people to learn about nature firsthand. A beautiful book! It totally changed the way we approached Nature Journals—the first day we looked at the book, my then 12-year-old daughter and I spent two hours at the local beaver pond sketching red-winged blackbirds, Canada geese, rough-skinned newts, turtles, and wildflowers.

Keep in mind that the easiest way to get kids to keep a Nature Notebook is for them to watch the example of their parent (you!) keeping a Nature Notebook of his or her own.

10

HOMESCHOOLING ON A BUDGET

Over the years, I've lost track of the number of times I've had new homeschooling moms cry on my shoulder about all the myriads of choices available for home education curriculum and supplies.

"We're just a struggling single income family! We can't afford all this awesome sounding stuff! But I want to give my children a rich and wonderful educational experience! What do I do?" Followed oftentimes by an audible sniffling.

Yep. I've cried those same tears, myself, a long time ago, especially when my kiddos were little and we were just starting down this lifestyle path.

When our children were first starting to be homeschooled, money was super tight in our family and I had to weigh carefully every purchase I made for our homeschooling. I learned a lot through those difficult financial times, one of the most important being that you don't need to spend much money at all to have a quality home educational experience for your family. Honestly, I think it's not just a quality education—I believe it's truly a superior education in many ways.

If I were at rock bottom financially and only had ten dollars to spend on curriculum for grades K-2, I would buy the small book, *The Three R's* by Ruth Beechick (it's a combination of what used to be three individual booklets). When my children were little, this simple little resource truly functioned as our core curriculum.

We also did relaxed nature study and kept casual nature notebooks. A stack of printer paper and some staples isn't as beautiful as an actual artist sketchbook, but it'll work in a pinch. We kept personal journals, too.

But basically we sat around for hours and hours and would read and read and read … and then we'd look at bugs and leaves and clouds … and we played in the sun for hours … and splashed in puddles … and built snowmen … and went to the free days at the art museum. And got to know the squirrels at the local park. And watched the leaves change through the seasons. And saw kittens being born. And made friends. And brought meals to sick neighbors. And lived our lives. We didn't do "school at home" per se—our home was our school. Does that make sense at all?

Life was simple, inexpensive, and wonderful.

So please don't cry, overwhelmed mom. You don't have to over schedule yourself, or over-plan your curriculum, or make sure everything's absolutely perfect, or spend hundreds of dollars on books, supplies, teacher's manuals, etc.

If I were a new mom just starting out with little ones and just beginning this homeschooling journey on a limited budget, I'd buy a copy of Ruth Beechick's *The Three R's* book mentioned earlier, and I'd read *For the Children's Sake* by Susan Schaeffer Macaulay for some Charlotte Mason inspiration. And also the older book, *Homeschooling for Excellence* by David and Micki Colfax as a reminder about how simple homeschooling can be and how educational real life actually is.

Other than that, I'd make sure the kiddos had pencils, crayons, pens, markers, lots of paper, a little tape and glue, and then I'd call it good.

There's plenty of time for hardcore academics and lesson plans and planned-out-curriculum and homeschool co-ops and all the other bells and whistles the well-meaning homeschool world will tell you that you need to do and buy and use to have a high-quality educational experience in your home. But you know what I think about all of that? Poppycock.

Here's what you actually need: One little book for curriculum. One or two for inspiration. Time, attention, fun, nature, and a library card. And really—take it from this mama who knows—that's all you need for the Second Grade and younger set.

Don't let anyone (including me!) guilt you into buying something you can't afford and probably don't need. Seriously, you can get all of this from the library. I recommend buying *The Three R's* because you'll be using it for several years and for any subsequent children, and I personally recommend buying a copy of *For the Children's Sake* because I've reread that particular book nearly every year for 20+ years to keep my vision for our homeschool fresh and clear. My original copy got so worn, I needed to buy a new one.

If you still feel like you just have to "do school" with your under-eight-year-old kiddos, please read the older book *Better Late than Early* by Raymond and Dorothy Moore. Do not pass go. Do not spend any money on curriculum, but do read this book as soon as possible. I believe it's an important step to fully get your mind around the fact that what we've been taught about when to start academics by the compulsory school systems is just plain wrong. *Better Late than Early* is based on research and not hearsay or somebody's thoughts about what would be nice or fun for kids.

Homeschool Curriculum Fair Warning

The random curriculum dealers and booksellers at homeschool conventions and curriculum fairs aren't really your friends. They're looking at you as a prospective sale. They're not bad people, mind you. They're business people with a product to sell. And homeschooling is big business these days. They might be perfectly nice people. And they probably are. They might be helpful and warm and friendly and appear to be everything you've ever wanted in a friend or mentor. And they probably are all of those things.

But remember, they're there to make a sale so they can make a profit. As you wander through the vendor aisles, you've become the latest target of their sales speech. Seriously. At the bare minimum, they need to make back the cost of renting that vendor space, table, or booth.

Because I'm including this brief section in this book, I don't expect any curriculum or book suppliers will be carrying it on their shelves. Oh, well. To be honest, I'd prefer not to sell any of these books at curriculum fairs, book sales, etc., if it means I can save other parents from making the same expensive mistakes I made, myself. In the early days of my homeschooling adventures, I found myself sometimes persuaded by fancy curriculum suppliers and homeschool conventions to try some new or flashy or wonderful "answer to all my homeschool woes." Somebody always appeared to have a new and improved "something" that seemed like it was just what I needed.

Oh, the weary life of a young homeschooling mom with little self-confidence. I wish I could go back to my younger self, give her a big hug, hold her hand, and help her withstand all those pressures to buy, buy, buy. I would say to her (and maybe to you?) as she's standing there overwhelmed with options and feeling like if she just had more money to throw at it, homeschooling would be perfect:

> "They're just trying to sell you something, Honey. Of course they're going to make it sound lovely and like it's the answer to whatever ails your homeschool. They're marketing to your insecurities. Go home now. Keep your money in your bank account, read a good book to your kiddos, take a walk in the park, feed the squirrels, and enjoy life together."

Now you, dear reader, go and do likewise.

11

SCHEDULING A CHARLOTTE MASON-STYLE DAY

A number of years ago, due to frequent requests from my regular web-page visitors, I wrote out a general outline and description of our family's daily homeschool schedule. Just so you know, this was written back when my oldest child was 12 years old. She's all grown up and married now.

At that time, I had our weekly schedule printed out as a chart for each child which I hung on the refrigerator at the beginning of each week. We marked off the subjects as we finished them and added notations of any specifics we needed to remember (page numbers read, art viewed, etc.) on little lines next to the space on the chart.

When reading through this day-by-day schedule, some people might think this is a lot to accomplish in any given day, but we were using Charlotte Mason's idea about short lessons (only ten to twenty minutes for each topic) so our academic part of the day only came out to around 3.5 hours per day.

I found my children enjoyed having a set task to accomplish in a set period of time. Since I'm not a particularly rigid person (I tend to go with the flow of life), I first thought this type of schedule would crimp my style—but I actually found it to be incredibly freeing. I was surprised.

With many school subjects, I found I could teach both of my older children at the same time by reading aloud to them together. Early on, my son wasn't reading fluently enough to gather much information from reading independently (he was still working on fluency and wasn't quite at the reading-for-knowledge stage).

My 12-year-old daughter did a great deal of independent work, so she did additional reading on the various topics we covered together as a group. Her independent reading time was followed by oral narrations for each subject (and occasionally written narrations).

The General Schedule

I was inspired to put together my own daily schedule after reading the books, *A Charlotte Mason Education* and *More Charlotte Mason Education* by Catherine Levison. The author had printed out samples of her own weekly schedules and also included examples of the actual schedules used in Charlotte Mason's schools back in the early 1900's (the schedules appeared in a December 1908 article in the Parent's Review).

While my family's homeschooling schedule was inspired by both Levison and Charlotte Mason, it by no means is representative of their actual schedules. This is simply how our family adapted the ideas to our own situation at the time.

MONDAY –

- Bible
- Memory Verse
- Reading
- Writing
- Spelling
- Math
- Literature
- Science
- Poetry

- P.E.
- Geography
- Recorder
- Crafts
- Drawing

TUESDAY –

- Bible
- Memory Verse
- Reading
- Writing
- Spelling
- Math
- Literature
- Science
- Poetry
- P.E.
- History
- Music Appreciation
- Art Appreciation'
- Home Economics
- Occupational Education

WEDNESDAY –

- Bible

- Memory Verse
- Reading
- Writing
- Spelling
- Math
- Literature
- Science
- Poetry
- P.E.
- Geography
- Recorder
- Crafts
- Drawing

THURSDAY –
1. Bible
2. Memory Verse
3. Reading
4. Writing
5. Spelling
6. Math
7. Literature
8. Science
9. Poetry
10. P.E.
11. History

12. Music Appreciation
13. Art Appreciation
14. Home Economics
15. Occupational Education

FRIDAY –

This was our less academic day.

- Moms' Group/Homeschool Group
- Volunteer opportunities
- Field trips
- Social activities
- And time to fill in any subjects that were skipped for whatever reason during the rest of the week

And then in addition to the day's schedule, every night at bedtime I would read to my children from their "just for fun" books—no official narration with these books except for a question when we first sat down. "So, what was happening in *Old Yeller* last night?"

I hope this brief overview of how we scheduled our homeschooling day when our kids were younger proves helpful to someone.

I've been told that Charlotte Mason encouraged teachers in her schools to come up with their own schedule of study each year to keep the various topics fresh for the teacher as well as for the student. But I find that many modern day Charlotte Mason homeschoolers want a bit more concrete guidance about what to study and when.

Numerous people I've talked with over the years—including myself—have found the Core Knowledge books by E. D. Hirsh to be a wonderful outline of what to study when (*What Your Kindergartener Needs to Know*, *What Your First Grader Needs to Know*, etc.). These home educators use the Core Knowledge books as their scope-and-sequence, and then flesh out the various topics with living books and use other Charlotte Mason techniques like narration, short lessons, and nature study to bring the curriculum alive.

12

TWADDLE-FREE READING LIST BY GRADE LEVEL

This reading list is simply my personal idea of twaddle-free reading—it isn't the Twaddle-free Gospel. Also, it's not a reading list of *must* reads or even *should* reads. This is just an example of *suggested* reads, so please don't feel your family needs to check off each book on this list.

Different families have different preferences and different sensitivities to topics, so each of our lists would probably look quite a bit different. This list is just to get you thinking about the types of books today that could be considered twaddle-free. Your mileage may vary.

- Living Books = books that are well-written and engaging—they absorb the reader—the narrative and characters seem to come alive; living books are the opposite of cold, dry textbooks.

- Twaddle = dumbed down literature; absence of meaning

Important Note about Age/Grade Listings

The age/grade designations for this list are only approximate. A child's listening level will often be several grades higher than their personal reading level—feel free to choose books from an older list if you're planning on reading aloud to your children. My husband and I began reading aloud to our children from chapter books (such as *Charlotte's Web*) before their third birthdays. Don't under-estimate your child's ability to comprehend fairly advanced material.

Preschool

- *Aesop's Fables*, illustrated by Jerry Pinkney
- *The Complete Tales of Peter Rabbit*, by Beatrix Potter
- *The Original Mother Goose*, illustrated by Blanche Fisher Wright
- *Good Night Moon*, by Margaret Wise Brown

- *The Runaway Bunny*, by Margaret Wise Brown
- *The Story of Babar, the Little Elephant*, by Jean de Brunhoff
- *The Very Hungry Caterpillar*, by Eric Carle
- *Where the Wild Things Are*, by Maurice Sendak

Kindergarten / Grade 1

- *Amelia Bedelia*, by Peggy Parish
- *Blueberries for Sal*, by Robert McCloskey
- *Bread and Jam for Frances*, by Russell Hoban
- *Billy and Blaze*, by C.W. Anderson
- *A Chair for My Mother*, by Vera B. Williams
- *Corduroy*, by Don Freeman
- *The Courage of Sarah Noble*, by Alice Dalgliesh
- *Curious George* books, by H.A. Rey
- *Frog and Toad* books, by Arnold Lobel
- *Harry the Dirty Dog*, by Gene Zion
- *Little Bear* books, by Else Homelund Minarik
- *The Little Engine that Could*, by Watty Piper
- *The Little House*, by Virginia Lee Burton
- *Madeline*, by Ludwig Bemelmans
- *Make Way for Ducklings*, by Robert McCloskey
- *Mike Mulligan and His Steam Shovel*, by Virginia Lee Burton

- *The Snowy Day*, by Ezra Jack Keats
- *Stone Soup*, by Marcia Brown
- *Story of Ferdinand*, by Munro Leaf
- *Story About Ping*, by Marjorie Flack

Grade 2

- *The Boxcar Children*, by Gertrude Chandler Warner
- *A Child's Garden of Verses*, by Robert Louis Stevenson
- *Little House on the Prairie* series, by Laura Ingalls Wilder
- *The Railway Children*, by E. Nesbit
- *The Random House Book of Fairy Tales*, by Amy Ehrlich
- *Tikki Tikki Tembo*, by Arlene Mosel
- *The Velveteen Rabbit*, by Marjery Williams
- *Winnie-the-Pooh* books, by A. A. Milne

Grade 3

- *Baby Island*, by Carol Ryrie Brink
- *Caddie Woodlawn*, by Carol Ryrie Brink

- *Charlotte's Web*, by E. B. White
- *Misty of Chincoteague*, by Marguerite Henry
- *Owls in the Family*, by Farley Mowat
- *Paul Bunyan*, by Steven Kellogg
- *Pollyanna*, by Eleanor H. Porter
- *Sarah, Plain and Tall*, by Patricia MacLachlan
- *Squanto, Friend of the Pilgrims*, by Clyde Robert Bulla
- *Story of Dr. Doolittle*, by Hugh Lofting
- *Stuart Little*, by E. B. White
- *Trumpet of the Swan*, by E. B. White

Grade 4

- *Alice in Wonderland*, by Lewis Carroll
- *Charlie and the Chocolate Factory*, by Roald Dahl
- *The Chronicles of Narnia*, by C. S. Lewis
- *King Arthur*, by Roger Lancelyn Green
- *A Little Princess*, by Frances Hodgson Burnett
- *Little Lord Fauntleroy*, by Frances Hodgson Burnett
- *The Phantom Tollbooth*, by Norton Juster
- *Pinocchio*, by Carlo Collodi
- *The Merry Adventures of Robin Hood*, by Howard Pyle

- *The Secret Garden*, by Frances Hodgson Burnett
- *Story of Rolf and the Viking Bow*, by Allen French
- *The Sword in the Stone*, by T.H. White
- *Tom Sawyer*, by Mark Twain
- *Twenty-One Balloons*, by William Pene du Bois
- *Redwall*, by Brian Jacques
- *The Wind in the Willows*, by Kenneth Grahame

Grade 5

- *Anne of Green Gables*, by L. M. Montgomery
- *Bambi: A Life in the Woods,* by Felix Salten
- *Black Beauty*, by Anna Sewell
- *Cheaper by the Dozen*, by Frank B. Gilbreth, Jr.
- *Gentle Ben*, by Walt Morey
- *Heidi*, by Johanna Spyri
- *Island of the Blue Dolphins*, by Scott O'Dell
- *Johnny Tremain*, by Esther Forbes
- *Lad: A Dog,* by Albert Payson Terhune
- *Old Yeller*, by Fred Gipson
- *Robinson Crusoe,* by Daniel Defoe
- *The Secret Garden,* by Frances Hodgson Burnett
- *The Swiss Family Robinson*, by Johann Wyss
- *Treasure Island*, by Robert Louis Stevenson

- *Where the Red Fern Grows*, by Wilson Rawls
- *The Witch of Blackbird Pond*, by Elizabeth George Speare

Grade 6

- *Around the World in Eighty Days*, by Jules Verne
- *The Call of the Wild*, by Jack London
- *A Christmas Carol*, by Charles Dickens
- *The Hobbit*, by J. R. R. Tolkien
- *Huckleberry Finn*, by Mark Twain
- *The Jungle Book*, by Rudyard Kipling
- *Just So Stories*, by Rudyard Kipling
- *Kidnapped*, by Robert Louis Stevenson
- *Little Women*, by Louisa May Alcott
- *White Fang*, by Jack London
- *The Yearling*, by Marjorie Kinnan Rawlings

Grade 7

- *Anne Frank: The Diary of a Young Girl*, by Anne Frank
- *Fahrenheit 451*, by Ray Bradbury
- *The Martian Chronicles*, by Ray Bradbury
- *Oliver Twist*, by Charles Dickens
- *The Pilgrim's Progress*, by John Bunyan

- *The Prince and the Pauper*, by Mark Twain
- *Sounder*, by William H. Armstrong
- *Tanglewood Tales*, by Nathaniel Hawthorne

Grade 8

- *Christy*, by Catherine Marshall
- *David Copperfield*, by Charles Dickens
- *The Divine Comedy*, by Dante
- *Don Quixote*, by Miguel de Cervantes
- *Emma*, by Jane Austen
- *The Great Divorce*, by C. S. Lewis
- *Paradise Lost*, by John Milton
- *Sir Gawain and the Green Knight*, by J. R. R. Tolkien

Younger High School

- *1984*, by George Orwell
- *The Best of Poe*, by Edgar Allen Poe
- *Brave New World*, by Aldous Huxley
- *The Chosen*, by Chaim Potok
- *Frankenstein*, by Mary Shelley
- *Jane Eyre*, by Charlotte Bronte
- *Les Miserables*, by Victor Hugo
- *Moby Dick*, by Herman Melville

- *The Old Man and the Sea*, by Ernest Hemmingway
- *The Pilgrim's Regress*, by C. S. Lewis
- *Pride and Prejudice*, by Jane Austen
- *The Strange Case of Dr. Jekyll and Mr. Hyde*, by Robert Louis Stevenson
- *Uncle Tom's Cabin*, by Harriet Beecher Stowe

Older High School

- *Animal Farm*, by George Orwell
- *A Tale of Two Cities*, by Charles Dickens
- *Ben Hur: A Tale of Christ*, by Lew Wallace
- *The Canterbury Tales*, by Geoffrey Chaucer
- *The City of God*, by Augustine
- *The Count of Monte Cristo*, by Alexandre Dumas
- *Great Expectations*, by Charles Dickens
- *The Great Gatsby*, by F. Scott Fitzgerald
- *Guilliver's Travels*, by Jonathan Swift
- *Hinds' Feet on High Places*, by Hannah Hurnard
- *The Last of the Mohicans*, by James Fenimore Cooper
- *The Lord of the Rings* (Trilogy), by J. R. R. Tolkien
- *The Odyssey*, by Homer
- *The Scarlet Letter*, by Nathaniel Hawthorne

- *The Scarlet Pimpernel*, by Baroness Emmuska Orczy
- *The Screwtape Letters*, by C. S. Lewis
- *Silas Marner*, by George Eliot
- *The Space Trilogy*, by C. S. Lewis
- *The Three Musketeers*, by Alexandre Dumas
- *To Kill a Mockingbird*, by Harper Lee

13

FRUGAL FAMILY FIELD TRIPS

Family field trips are a simple, fun, and fairly inexpensive educational enrichment activity you can enjoy regularly with your children. Here are some quick ideas to get you started.

- Many manufacturing plants offer free tours to families or small groups. Any free samples given out make great souvenirs when on vacation. Call ahead to find out about tour availability.

- Field trips to local attractions such as zoos or aquariums can be expensive, but purchasing an annual family pass pays for itself in just a couple of trips. Knowing you can come back again and again, frees your family to relax and enjoy themselves without feeling pressured to hurry and see everything in one day to get your money's worth out of the admission price. Return to the same site whenever you want a family outing, and then buy a pass to a different educational attraction next year.

- If your family enjoys attending live performances, check for free concerts, plays and other cultural events in local parks during the summer months.

- You can also contact college or community performance groups (drama, ballet, orchestra, etc.) to see if they'll allow you to watch them rehearse for free.

- Many local theater groups need volunteer ushers for their live performances. Volunteering in this manner is an excellent way for the older members of your family to gain free admission to a wide variety of cultural events, plus it provides a useful service to the local arts community.

14

TWADDLE-FREE HOLIDAYS

One year in the midst of the December holidays, I chatted at length with Catherine Levison (author of *A Charlotte Mason Education* and *More Charlotte Mason Education*). Catherine and I got together to come up with ways to apply the concept of avoiding twaddle (or what modern parents might call "dumbed down" literature and activities) in our holiday celebrations, family times, and celebratory reading materials.

Defining Twaddle in Literature

First, let's look at the synonyms of twaddle which include: babble, drivel and silly. Ordinarily twaddle refers to literature written down to children. Books written specifically to children are not avoided.

A good example would be any of Beatrix Potter's works—she wrote to children but not down to them. Or the original A. A. Milne *Winnie-the-Pooh* books are another good example of twaddle-free just-for-fun children's reading material.

Regarding children's literature, look for interesting content and well-constructed sentences clothed in literary language. The imagination should be warmed and the book should hold the interest of the child. Life's too short to spend time with books that bore us. If our children have only been exposed to junk food, they may resist trying nutritious food. If they've been raised on twaddle, they may need to be weaned slowly off this mental junk food. Ideally, if they were not exposed to twaddly books in the first place, all involved would be way ahead of the game.

It's our opinion that dumbed-down literature is easy to spot. When you're standing in the library and pick up modern-day, elementary-level books, you're apt to see short sentences with very little effort applied to artistically constructing them to please the mind. Almost anyone can write—but not everyone is gifted in this field. Gifted authors bring images alive with their choice of words. Gifted authors often write classic literature, and classics are an excellent way to spend one's reading time.

Twaddle is easy to come by; the planet is filled with it. People coped with it in previous centuries, and we must cope with it in ours. If anything, literature has deteriorated even further. The best way to handle this excessive quantity of bad books is to stand firm and only spend our money on the best—even at holiday time.

But what about friends and relatives who unknowingly supply our children with twaddle at gift-giving times? Try talking to those who are apt to buy gifts for your children and tell them about the direction you're heading with reading material. Some people pick up on things easier than others, therefore, for some folks a simple explanation of the type of literature you want purchased as gifts is all they'll need.

If you've started to collect any particular set of children's classics currently in bookstores or catalogues, you could provide Grandma with a list of titles you'd like. Be specific, and offer to help her with the ordering or perhaps even drive her to your favorite bookstore.

Twaddle-Free Holidays

How else can we apply the concept of twaddle to the holiday season as a whole? I firmly believe that twaddle is in the eye of the beholder. That means some of the following ideas may appeal to you while others may not meet your expectations. Catherine and I put our heads together and came up with the following ideas—some of which were shared with us over the years by other people. As always, take what you like and ignore what you don't.

During the holidays, I frequently discover a large number of low-cost entertainment options by reading the "What's Happening" section of our local newspaper. For example, during one holiday season, I discovered a listing for a singing group performing traditional Celtic holiday carols at a local church for just a small donation. Many churches and community groups put on low-cost (or free) live performances during the holidays.

Rather than taking the family to a newly released holiday movie, consider spending a few extra dollars and attend a ballet or classical concert instead. Many times attending a concert by a local symphony performing familiar Christmas songs is a very child-friendly introduction to symphonic music for children who haven't previously experienced that type of music. Also, many churches offer sing-a-longs of Handel's Messiah that are open to the general public.

As we all know, holiday music is drastically varied. Perhaps some attention to playing classical music around the house—while avoiding animated cartoon characters screeching their holiday favorites—would be more soothing.

Many families, including both Catherine's and my own, buy one new Christmas book each year and have the holiday book collection on display. Catherine's favorite Christmas book is called *The Christmas Story* featuring the paintings of Gennady Spirin. It's breathtakingly beautiful and priced accordingly— however Catherine insists it's worth every penny. This is one way to include masterpiece artwork into this season of the year.

It's also time to buy next year's calendar. If you haven't thought of it before, hold out until you find one featuring fine art rather than kittens, horses or cars. Along with being a practical item, the calendars often provide excellent prints to use for art appreciation throughout the year.

While grown children and other relatives visit, provide some old-fashioned fun that can be enjoyed by young and old alike. Charades, sing-a-longs, board games and caroling are easy, affordable and fun. Catherine's family collects Christmas jigsaw puzzles— which may appear to be a bit twaddly at first glance— but they truly enjoy spending time together which makes it more than an aimless pursuit. You could also choose puzzles depicting masterpieces or popular works of art.

Many families are constructing their own advent calendars (from wood or paper) and incorporating photographs and other touches. If everyone in the family participates in a project of this sort, then they can all look forward to getting it out each December.

Are you dreaming of a white Christmas? Well, if the snow doesn't come to you then go to the snow. Some folks make an annual trek to the mountains during December in order to be assured of some contact with winter weather.

Obviously, there are countless good ideas that help families enjoy each other.

15

THE ADVENT BOOK BOX

A great idea for the holidays is to set aside a special box or basket containing your family's special Christmas and other holiday books. The Holiday (or Advent) Book Box only comes out during the Advent season, and is put away again with the decorations after the first of the year.

The following list is favorite Christmastime books compiled many years ago following a discussion between a group of homeschooling mothers looking for twaddle-free holiday reading for their families. The out-of-print titles are often available used through online booksellers and auction sites such as Amazon.com, eBay.com, and ABEbooks.com

- *A Christmas Carol,* by Charles Dickens

- *Becky's Christmas*, by Tasha Tudor (out-of-print)
- *(The) Best Christmas Pageant Ever!* by Barbara Robinson
- *Christmas at Long Pond*, by William T. George (out-of-print)
- *(The) Christmas Box*, by Richard Paul Evans
- *(The) Christmas Miracle of Jonathan Toomey*, by Susan Wojciechowski
- *(The) Christmas Stories of George MacDonald*, by George MacDonald (out-of-print)
- *(The) Christmas Tree*, by Julie Salamon
- *(The) Crippled Lamb*, by Max Lucado
- *(The) Donkey's Dream*, by Barbara Helen Berger
- *(The) First Christmas*, by Marcia Williams (out-of-print)
- *(The) Glorious Impossible*, by Madeleine L'Engle (out-of-print)
- *Martin Luther's Christmas Book*, by Martin Luther
- *(The) Night Before Christmas by Clement Moore*, illustrated by Jan Brett
- *A Northern Nativity: Christmas Dreams of a Prairie Boy*, by William Kurelek
- *One Wintry Night*, by Ruth Bell Graham
- *Rembrandt: The Christmas Story*

- *Seven Stories of Christmas Love*, by Leo F. Buscaglia
- *(The) Story of Christmas: Words from the Gospels of Matthew and Luke*, illustrated by Jane Ray
- *Tale of Three Trees*, by Angela Elwell Hunt
- *This is the Star*, by Joyce Dunbar

16

INDOOR WINTER BOREDOM BUSTERS

Since we tried not to use the phrase "I'm bored!" in our home, I usually didn't hear my kids complaining about being bored during those long days at home during the winter. But I have to admit that we were still an incredibly normal family. Even without the "b-word" in their vocabulary, there were still those times when my three children just seemed to be at a total loss for something constructive to do.

Many years ago I brainstormed with my kids and some of our assorted friends and we came up with a list of 200+ ideas for summertime activities. I decided to narrow the list down to just those things that can be done indoors and aren't weather-dependent for those cold snowy days home from school or during winter vacation times.

You can put each item on this list onto individual pieces of paper, place the papers into a container, and when the children need inspiration for an activity, they can draw out two or three papers and then decide which idea they want to do, either as a group or individually. This method is usually more helpful than giving the kids a huge list of possibilities. By narrowing the choices down to just two or three, it's easier for the kids to pick out the one that sounds the best to them.

Indoor Boredom Busters:

- make paper snowflakes
- clean out the toy box
- send virtual greeting cards
- choose photos for a family calendar
- have an indoor picnic
- bake and decorate cut-out cookies
- go camping in the livingroom
- clear out your email inbox
- make a mobile out of found objects (acorns, rocks, branches)
- write up some New Year's Resolutions
- create a simple Family Tree
- make sandwiches and cut them out with large cookie cutters

- play basketball with a wadded up piece of paper and a wastebasket
- play board games
- make a tent out of blankets
- read books
- make homemade play dough
- play with play dough
- write a letter to a relative, friend or pen pal
- clean bedroom
- vacuum living room
- clean bathroom
- make a craft
- draw
- color
- paint
- watch a movie
- write stories
- use magnifying glass
- write a play
- act out a play
- invent indoor circus acts
- perform an indoor circus
- play card games
- dust the house
- brush the pet

- write letters
- read a magazine
- play dress-up
- build a fort in your rooms
- do a jigsaw puzzle
- play on the Geo-Safari or other educational game
- play on the computer
- listen to a story or book on tape
- do extra schoolwork to get ahead
- do brain teasers (ie: crosswords, word searches, hidden pictures, mazes, etc.)
- cook
- prepare lunch
- surprise a neighbor with a good deed
- play store
- prepare a "restaurant" lunch with menus
- hold a tea party
- have a Teddy bear picnic on the floor in the living room
- play with toy cars
- play dolls
- play house
- learn magic tricks
- put on a magic show

- make sock puppets
- put on a puppet show
- crochet or knit
- make doll clothes
- sew buttons in designs on old shirts
- make bookmarks
- take a quiet rest time
- take a shower or bath
- organize a dresser drawer
- clean under the bed
- empty dishwasher
- vacuum under the couch cushions and keep any change found
- write these ideas on pieces of paper and pick out one or two to do
- practice musical instruments
- perform a family concert
- teach yourself to play a musical instrument (recorder, harmonica, guitar)
- fold laundry
- sweep kitchen or bathroom floors
- vacuum or dust window blinds
- clean bathroom mirrors
- clean sliding glass doors
- copy your favorite book illustration

- design your own game
- build with blocks or Legos™
- create a design box (copper wire, string, odds-and-ends of things destined for the garbage, pom-poms, thread, yarn, etc.)
- have a marble tournament on the living room carpet
- make dessert
- make dinner
- give your pet a party
- have a read-a-thon with a friend or sibling
- check out a science book and try some experiments
- make up a story
- arrange photo albums
- play hide-and-seek
- create a symphony with bottles and pans and rubber bands
- read a story to a younger child
- string dry noodles or O-shaped cereals into a necklace
- glue noodles into a design on paper
- play jacks
- make up a song
- make an indoor teepee out of blankets
- write in your journal

- play charades
- make up a story by drawing pictures
- draw a cartoon strip
- make a map of your bedroom, house or neighborhood
- call a friend
- cut pictures from old magazines and write a story
- make a collage using pictures cut from old magazines
- plan a treasure hunt
- make a treasure map
- make up a "Bored List" of things to do
- plan a special activity for your family
- search your house for items made in other countries and then learn about those countries from the encyclopedia or online
- plan an imaginary trip to the moon
- plan an imaginary trip around the world, where would you want to go?
- write a science-fiction story
- find a new pen pal
- make up a play using old clothes as costumes
- make up a game for practicing math facts
- have a Spelling Bee
- make up a game for practicing spelling

- write newspaper articles for a pretend newspaper
- put together a family newsletter
- write reviews of movies or plays or TV shows or concerts you see during the break from school
- bake a cake
- bake a batch of cookies
- decorate a shoe box
- make a hideout or clubhouse
- make paper airplanes
- have paper airplane races
- learn origami
- make friendship bracelets for your friends
- make a wind chime out of things headed for the garbage
- paint your face
- braid hair
- play tag
- make food sculptures (from pretzels, gumdrops, string licorice, raisins, cream cheese, nuts, nut butter, etc.) and then eat it
- produce a talent show
- memorize a poem
- recite a memorized poem for your family

Have fun!

17

WINTER EDUCATIONAL IDEAS FOR PRESCHOOLERS

It's always fun to use things in our children's everyday lives to spark discussion and easy educational activities. The current season can be a great topic of study for our littlest ones. Study time with preschoolers at home mainly consists of talking and laughing with them, helping them notice the details of the world around them. No pressure. Just a fun time spent in the company of a loving adult.

To introduce the topic of Winter, ask your child what she knows about the seasons. Is she aware of spring, summer, autumn, and winter? Does she know what the differences are between the seasons in your local area?

Don't lecture. Just make conversation and find out what she knows already. Have her look out the window and tell you what she notices about the trees, bushes, flowers and gardens. Are there leaves visible? Buds? Flowers? Greenery? Bare branches? Brown stems?

Find a photo, painting, or picture in a book of an obvious winter scene. Ask your child if she knows what season it is in the picture. What things tell her what time of year it is? If she doesn't know, point things out to her that will give clues: bare branches, snow on the ground, no flowers, people in warm clothes, etc. Hide the picture from view and have the child describe to you in her own words what she saw in the picture. Encourage as much detail as possible, but remember to keep it low-key and fun. This process of orally telling back what she's seen helps cement the image in her memory.

To supplement your discussion, enjoy together a winter-time picture book such as Ezra Jack Keat's *The Snowy Day* or the Alaskan tale *Momma, Do You Love Me?* by Barbara M. Joosse.

Ask your child how people stay warm in the winter (warm clothes, mittens, fireplaces, warm houses, etc.). Let her brainstorm for a while. Then ask how she thinks animals stay warm in winter (thick fur, migrate to warmer climates, hibernate in caves, etc.).

Sometimes a preschool child might say things like, "Baby squirrels snuggle up in a tree with a soft blanket to stay warm." Ask her gently if she's ever seen a real squirrel with a blanket. Does she think that's how they'll really stay warm in those cold, winter months? The line between fantasy and reality in preschoolers is sometimes thin. Don't harshly bring your child into reality, just gently coax her into thinking about how things really happen in nature. But just so you don't think it all needs to be a serious dose of reality, have some fun and brainstorm about "pretend" ways animals might stay warm. For fun, read one of these wonderfully fun and beautifully illustrated winter-time books by Jan Brett (one of my favorite children's illustrators):

- *The Mitten*
- *The Hat*

You can also visit Jan Brett's website to print out coloring sheets and other fun projects based on Brett's lavishly illustrated children's books: Janbrett.com

For a fun activity, throw a collection of clothing and accessories into a bag or suitcase. Without looking, have your child reach into the bag, pull out a single clothing item and then tell you if the item they grabbed is appropriate to wear in the winter. Have the child explain to you why each item is—or isn't—seasonally appropriate. Include a variety of things in the bag such as: a warm hat, a pair of gloves or mittens, an open-toed sandal, a swimsuit, summer shorts, a warm sweater, a snow boot, a woolen scarf, a sleeveless top, etc.

Have your child finish the sentence, "Winter is." For example: Winter is "cold"; winter is "snowmen"; winter is "mittens"; winter is "hot cocoa and marshmallows." Consider writing down your child's responses. She'll feel so official seeing her words written down on paper. If you're feeling particularly creative, you can even print out little "Winter is …" booklets using family photos or clip-art found on your computer coinciding with your child's responses. Or have your child hand-illustrate their own homemade "Winter is … " booklet. Or let her cut out winter photos from magazines and newspapers, pasting them onto a large sheet of paper as a "Winter is …" collage.

Have a wonderful time as you explore the glories of the seasons with your preschooler.

18

INTERVIEW WITH THE AUTHOR

Over the years, I've been interviewed numerous times for various online and print publications about our homeschooling journey. I recently pooled together my responses from several different interviews because people kept asking for "my story" about how we homeschooled and why.

---

1) What was your first impression of the concept of homeschooling?

I first heard about homeschooling in the early 1980's. I worked with a man whose family was homeschooling. I'd never heard of the concept and my first knee-jerk response was, "Oh my gosh! How horrible!" I valued education so highly that I thought it was bordering on negligence to not send kids to a school building each day. Silly me. At the time, I was equating school with education. But I learned otherwise soon enough.

---

2) Why did you decide to home educate your children?

The story of my homeschooling co-worker and his family continued. I grilled that poor guy almost non-stop whenever we had time at work just to chat. Fortunately, he was calm and incredibly reasonable about all my questions. Almost before I knew it, I had an "Ah ha!" moment and realized that one-on-one tutoring was the single best style of educating someone and that tutoring was essentially what homeschooled students would get every day of their lives throughout their educational career.

With that one sudden flash of insight, I became a dyed-in-the-wool home education believer. And this was before my husband and I even had children of our own! It would be another four years before we had our first baby.

I feel I can honestly say we've homeschooled from birth because we knew long before we even had kids that we would home educate, and I started researching educational methods way back then.

3) What is your family situation (married, single, how many kids, working mom, etc.) and how does this affect your homeschooling?

I've been married to my husband for 35 years, although he had to move out ten years ago when he was diagnosed with a degenerative brain disorder, and it became unsafe for him to remain in the home with us. I'm essentially a single (though still married) mom of three adults.

All three children lived at home after graduating high school in order to save money while they were in college. My oldest daughter is now married, my son moved out recently, and now it's just my youngest daughter and I at home (plus our beloved cats and bunnies).

I work as much as I can from home doing freelance writing and promoting my books and web-resources. I also pick up hours as I can at local businesses. I've worked full-time through the holidays at a Customer Service Call Center, for example.

While the kids were young, I was a stay-at-home mom. Homeschooling was easy back then, but difficult, too, because money was super tight. I learned to keep our homeschooling expenses as low as possible, and even ended up writing several books on living frugally as a result of our family's lean financial times.

After my husband's diagnoses and the subsequent loss of the majority of our family's income, I've never stopped the whole frugal thing. I found my kids were always willing to do odd jobs and find part-time work to provide for their own spending money——which was probably an education in itself for them. They have a great appreciation for the simple things in life, and never take for granted even the most normal things.

---

4) What method or approach to homeschooling do you use?

We've used a combination of Charlotte Mason's methods and unschooling. I was inspired early on by the books *Homeschooling for Excellence* by the Colfax family (unschooling), *For the Children's Sake* by Susan Schaeffer Macaulay (Charlotte Mason), and *Better Late Than Early* by Raymond and Dorothy Moore. We usually did our Charlotte Mason studies in the morning and unschooled in the afternoon (although there was often a lot of overlap).

I returned to college and finished my degree. In one of my classes, I wrote a research paper about which homeschooling methods are most effective depending on what results you want to see in your children. You can read my paper in the last section of this book: "Are All Homeschooling Methods Created

Equal?"

---

5) Have you always used this approach?

The only time I ever tried anything different was the very first year of Kindergarten for my oldest daughter. I guess I was feeling insecure about teaching my own kids, so I purchased the complete Kindergarten package from Calvert School. I felt it was the program that best fit with Charlotte Mason ideals at the time (there weren't a lot of curriculum options back then).

Much to my surprise, my daughter had already learned everything in the entire Kindergarten curriculum just through us living our lives naturally and educating organically. Rather than feeling I'd wasted my money on that year's curriculum, I always felt it was the best money I ever spent on homeschooling because it bought me confidence in my abilities to teach my own. Never bought another box of curriculum again.

---

6) What are the advantages of this method you've seen in your family's homeschooling?

As I was already committed to home education

when I first read *For the Children's Sake* (my introduction to Charlotte Mason), the book helped to cement my dreams and visions for our family, and gave me reassurance that I, as my children's mother, could provide—not just an adequate education—but a rich and full educational experience for my children.

I can honestly say that my children have grown into thoughtful, strong, ethical adults. Their home education has them well-prepared for college. Critical thinking is second nature to them. They're not peer-dependent. They've each been able to pursue their individual passions fully (social sciences, philosophy, art) which is something they probably wouldn't have had time for in a regular school setting or even in a more traditional textbook or curriculum-based home school.

---

7) What has been your homeschooling philosophy or objective?

I've always been a big fan of Charlotte Mason's educational philosophies and have attempted to apply them to our homeschooling efforts. Charlotte Mason developed a lifetime love of learning in her students by engaging the children firsthand with nature, literature, science, history, art, music, and avoiding dumbed-down materials as much as possible. The main focus of Mason's educational ideas and philosophy was having the students read top quality literature—real books rather than textbooks—and delving into a wide variety of serious topics throughout childhood. Mason described most literature written to children as "twaddle" and felt that childish materials should be avoided at all costs.

8) For those who don't know, who was Charlotte Mason?

Charlotte Mason was a British educator from the early part of the last century. Her methods and philosophies have recently experienced a resurgence—especially among American homeschooling families. Her emphasis on developing a lifetime love of learning was in stark contrast to the almost anti-child climate of her time. In response to her own experience and education, she conducted lectures, wrote numerous books on educational topics, founded a school for training governesses and others working with children in her methods, and published a monthly periodical called The Parents' Review which allowed her to stay in touch with her followers throughout the country (and the world). Eventually the Parents' Union Schools based on her philosophies sprung up throughout England and her training school became a college to supply teachers for the Parents' Union Schools.

9) Are Charlotte Mason's philosophies still relevant today, in the 21st Century?

I believe Charlotte Mason's basic philosophies are timeless. Developing a lifetime love of learning is something that's never out of date. The mission of my website, A Charlotte Mason-Style Home Education, is to bring Charlotte Mason's ideas and methods to modern families.

I believe that Mason's teachings are timeless, and I'm definitely not afraid to move those ideas out of the past and into the modern age. While I enjoy Victorian decor as much as the next person, I believe Charlotte Mason would've made use of every modern convenience, development, and scientific method available. She was considered a bit *avant garde* in her day and surely would have today, as well.

---

10) When starting to home educate the Charlotte Mason way, what do you think should be the focus?

For someone new to Charlotte Mason's methods and philosophies, I would recommend they start out by focusing on finding good twaddle-free books to read.

Charlotte Mason also had much to say

on establishing good habits in children. She believed that habits (good or bad) are like the ruts in a path from a wheelbarrow going down the same trail again and again. As time goes on, it becomes increasingly difficult to run the wheelbarrow outside the rut, but the wheel will always run smoothly down the well-worn rut in the path. By training children in good habits, the school day (and home life in general) goes more smoothly. Focus on one habit at a time for 4-6 weeks rather than attempting to implement a long list of new habits all at once. I would also focus on Nature Study.

If someone has only just recently been introduced to Charlotte Mason's ideas but has already purchased this year's books or curriculum, don't fret or worry. You really don't have to throw out your entire curriculum or all of those expensive textbooks (at least not yet).

---

11) How did you spend most of your homeschooling time?

While we were actively homeschooling, we spent the most time reading aloud together from books (classic literature, history, philosophy, geography, etc.), doing Nature Study (taking nature walks, keeping nature notebooks, visiting zoos, etc.), and we were also actively engaged in our local community.

We also continually practiced Narration, which is essentially just retelling what you've heard, seen or experienced—thus cementing the learning process. The whole idea of narration made sense to me right away because I saw how natural it was to want to tell someone about a good book or a fun movie, and then in the retelling, the story seemed to come alive all over again, living in the memory in a new way because of the retelling. I also saw clearly that if someone knew they would have to retell something they've read or seen, they'd listen intently.

For a number of years, we followed a schedule that really helped to keep us on track.

As my children launched into their college studies, I would say that their intensive experience with narrating throughout their homeschooling years was the single best thing we did to prepare them for college-level reading, writing, and thinking. My children never thought of narration as some sort of official school thing we did. They've often told me that they just thought of narration as "Mom's funny game" we'd play every day.

---

12) What types of books or curriculum did you use in your home school?

A TWADDLE-FREE EDUCATION

We didn't use a lot of actual curriculum per se, but pieced together our own from books in our home (we have 2,000+ books on our shelves now!), from free book texts online, and from our local public library.

Rather than purchasing a curriculum or teacher's manual of some sort, I've used the *What Your First Grader Needs to Know* (and others in the Core Knowledge series by E. D. Hirsh) as our basic scope-and-sequence of what to learn and when from Kindergarten through sixth grade. I supplemented the readings and information in those books with twaddle-free "living" whole books

---

13) What types of activities were your children involved with outside your home school?

Over the years my children were involved in both formal and informal cooperative types of groups and classes with other homeschoolers (science, history, Moms/kids groups, camps). They were involved with writing, editing and publishing a newsletter with a group of unschoolers from our community for several years. We studied a number of short stories with some friends. My kids all took ballet. There have been music lessons, a neighborhood 4-H Club, nature camps, Vacation Bible School, and the list goes on and on.

Who says homeschoolers aren't socialized? Sometimes I felt I needed to guard against too much socializing! I usually limited my kids to one activity of their own each season so I wasn't driving all over town all the time. I wanted to homeschool, not car school.

A lot of the outside things we did were things everyone could be involved in at the same time. For example, when my younger two were attending a local nature camp, my oldest daughter and I volunteered as camp leaders.

Other than a science/history co-op we did with four other families for a year, I never really liked using the local homeschooling cooperatives that were springing up. I found that the other parents really didn't understand the direction I was going with my homeschooling. It seemed to me they were basically recreating a traditional classroom setting for their kids (which was actually what I was trying to avoid through homeschooling).

I wasn't motivated to homeschool from a desire to shelter my kids like many of the other homeschooling parents I was meeting back then. I was motivated mainly by educational and philosophical goals which sometimes put me at odds with the powers-that-be in local homeschooling support groups. So I usually just ended up forming my own groups, usually pretty casual and easy-going groups, with other like-minded home educators. I guess I've always been a bit of a rebel and willing to forge my own path and avoid going-with-the-crowd.

---

14) What was your biggest challenge of homeschooling high school students?

Probably the biggest challenge of homeschooling high school students for me was letting go of the fear of whether or not they were learning what they needed to be learning. With my first high school student, we used the fairly free-form version of Clonlara School's home study program. Clonlara can work with any style of study (from textbooks to unschooling) and the student comes out of it all with an official high school diploma.

It was a great program and I highly recommend it, especially if you need an official diploma for some reason. It's also a great option if you have extended family members who are concerned about your ability to educate your older kids. Just being able to say my daughter was enrolled in a "real" school and that we were in contact with a "real" teacher seemed to set all the naysayers at ease.

Also, by using the Clonlara program with one child, it had a similar effect as buying that Calvert curriculum for Kindergarten years before. My confidence grew by leaps and bounds, and I also learned a lot about record keeping and what constitutes a solid high school education.

My younger two kiddos both graduated from our home school without using Clonlara—a testimony to my increased confidence as a teacher, but also a result of becoming essentially a single mom and having to survive on a super limited income after it became necessary for my husband to live separately from us. There was just no money for paying for a program like Clonlara anymore. I'm glad I had Clonlara for one student, though, so my confidence level was prepared for the difficult next stage of life that was coming to our family.

---

15) What has homeschooling taught you about yourself and your children?

I've learned that even though my kids all have the same biological and social background, they're each very much individuals. I'm so glad they were home educated so they were able to bloom into their full potential without someone trying to place them into an educational or social box that wouldn't have fit any of them.

I've also learned that I can trust my own instincts. Sometimes I would find myself comparing my laid back, casual homeschooling approach to some of my textbook and curriculum friends and wonder if my kids were missing something. But I kept reminding myself that it didn't matter what other people were doing. What mattered was what I was doing, and if it was successfully working out with my children and our family.

I also noticed that many of my more traditional homeschooling friends were burning out by high school, and then sending their kids off to the local public or private high school, even if they personally didn't believe in sending their kids away to school. I thought that was sad. I can honestly say I never felt burnt out.

My children developed a lifetime love of learning, and I developed a lifetime love of teaching. I returned to college at the same times as my oldest daughter and completed my Bachelor of Arts (Interdisciplinary Arts & Science: Literature focus), and I began Graduate School in September 2014 (Master of Fine Arts in Creative Writing & Poetics). My long term goal is to teach at a community college or university and to start a writing center and tutoring service for elementary through high school students based on Charlotte Mason principles.

16) Finish this sentence: "Homeschooling is …"

Homeschooling is the single greatest choice I've

made in my life and has allowed my children (and me, too!) to grow and flourish, even in the midst of some difficult life challenges.

19

RESEARCH: ARE ALL HOMESCHOOLING METHODS CREATED EQUAL?

Are All Homeschooling Methods Created Equal?
Copyright 2010 Deborah Taylor-Hough

In his provocative essay, "Against School," John Taylor Gatto (2003) details many of the problems he sees with America's public schools and methods of education. Gatto (2003) quotes H. L. Mencken in The American Mercury that "(t)he aim of public education is not to spread enlightenment at all; it is simply to reduce as many individuals as possible to the same safe level, to breed and train a standardized citizenry, to down dissent and originality." As a former New York State Teacher of the Year, Gatto's views of public education were developed after years of firsthand experience within the very system he critiques. When receiving his Teacher of the Year award, Gatto said, "We live in a time of great school crisis. We rank at the bottom of 19 industrialized nations in reading, writing, and arithmetic. At the very bottom" (Taylor, 2009).

In "Against School," Gatto tells his readers what he sees as the cure for the situation of today's schools. He would like to see parents counteract the effect of the schools by teaching their children 1) to be leaders and adventurers, 2) to think critically and independently, 3) to have a well-developed inner thought life, 4) to spend time alone learning to enjoy their own company, and 5) to interact with adult-level books and materials in a wide range of subjects covering the Liberal Arts and Sciences (Gatto, 2003).

After reading Gatto's bold statements in "Against School," concerned parents could quickly make the assumption that home educating their children is the best solution; dashing out to their local teachers' supply store to stock up on workbooks, textbooks, and flashcards. Homeschooling may not be the right choice for many families, but what about those parents who feel that—for their family and their situation—home education is the best option? They need to ask themselves before venturing into this new lifestyle: Are all homeschooling methods and materials created equal?

If the parents' goal is to educate their children in a manner that will bring about Gatto's goals for parents as outlined in "Against School," will the fact that children are now sitting around their kitchen table with their siblings rather than sitting at a school desk surrounded by their peers ultimately make that much of a difference in the more subjective educational outcomes of these children, as outlined by Gatto, if the educational methods chosen are the same as those employed in the schools?

If parents decide that it is not just the location of their children's schooling that matters, but also the method(s) used, then it becomes necessary to identify which of the home education methods commonly employed by homeschooling families would most likely produce the results Gatto desires, such as maturity, independence, and creative critical thinking. Based on Gatto's description of a well-educated person, a combination of two commonly used homeschooling methods—the Charlotte Mason method and unschooling—would most likely produce the results Gatto would like to see in students.

Brief Homeschooling Overview

The history of home education is long and varied. In her book, *Homeschoolers' Success Stories*, Linda Dobson (2000) states, "The current homeschooling movement is only new in that it has occurred following compulsory attendance laws and has grown sizeable enough to be noticed." Prior to those compulsory attendance laws enacted throughout the United States—starting with Massachusetts in 1852 until the 48th state, Mississippi, joined the rest of the country's compulsory attendance legislation in 1918 (Gatto, 2000)—most children were either educated at home, learned a trade through apprenticeships or personal mentoring, or were sent to private schools if their parents had the financial means to do so.

In 2007, an estimated 1.5 million children in the United States were being homeschooled and research found that "parents homeschooled their children for a variety of reasons, but three reasons—to provide religious or moral instruction, concern about the school environment, and dissatisfaction with the academic instruction at other schools—were noted as most important" (National Center for Education Statistics, 2008).

While homeschooling represents an increasingly broad cross-section of American families, there is still on-going conflict and disagreement existing between the secular and the religious-motivated homeschoolers, and also between the adherents of various educational methods and philosophies (Dobson, 2000).

Catherine Levison—author of *A Charlotte Mason Education: A Homeschooling How-to Manual* and frequent keynote speaker to homeschooling conventions throughout the United States—listed the main forms of home education she sees in home schools across America today: Unschooling, Classical education, unit studies, the Charlotte Mason method, traditional school-at-home, correspondence schools and school-related umbrella organizations, cooperatives, and computer-based options (Levison, personal communication, 2010). These methods and the expected outcomes of each as they relate to Gatto's article will be explored in more depth later in this paper.

Literature Review:
Homeschooling's History, Motivations, and Outcomes

The history of modern homeschooling has its roots in the counterculture Liberal Left, but within twenty years, the movement was fully adopted by the equally counterculture Conservative Right. The ideologies and methodologies surrounding these two diverse and oftentimes polarized groups created an interesting mix of people and cultures within the homeschooling world. Scholarly research and studies on the topic of homeschooling tend to be somewhat limited by the lack of direct availability to homeschooled students. Local school districts receive no funding for homeschoolers in their districts and are not required to keep or report information about homeschoolers to any government agencies, limiting research results to homeschool families self-reporting.

The academic achievement levels in outcome-focused studies are based on results from standardized achievement tests, so consequently any home educator who may choose not to participate in these tests for philosophical, ideological, or pedagogical reasons is excluded from these results. Standardized tests also fail to measure more subjective outcomes such as maturity level, personal autonomy, and creative critical thinking which Gatto hoped to see parents instilling in their children (Gatto, 2003).

History of Modern Homeschooling

In the early 1960's, John Holt, a prominent educator, humanist and author, advocated for radical school reform in his popular books, *How Children Fail* and *How Children Learn*. Holt stressed in his writings the need for "educational decentralization and greater parental autonomy" (Wilhelm & Firmin, 2009, p. 307). At the same time as Holt's work, many of the 1960's "hippies" were moving into communes, having babies, and hesitating to send their children to the local government-run ("too Conservative") schools. According to Wilhelm and Firmin (2009), the original modern day homeschoolers were part of the free-love hippy communes of the 1960's (p. 307).

In the 1970's, Holt was contacted by several counterculture Liberal Left homesteaders who were living remotely throughout the countryside, educating their children off the compulsory education grid (Gaither, 2008, p. 125). Holt decided to connect these independent and relatively isolated families with one another, and in 1977, began publishing Growing Without Schooling (GWS), the first newsletter dedicated solely to home schoolers. GWS became a way for these families to share wisdom and knowledge with each other, and to find moral support from others who had also chosen this radical means of schooling (or "unschooling") their children. Through his tireless activism, Holt—almost by accident—became the *de facto* leader of the then-underground and mostly illegal homeschooling movement (Gaither, 2008, p. 126). Homeschooling did not become legal in all fifty states until 1993 (Wilhelm & Firmin, 2009, p. 309).

Eventually, Holt connected with Raymond and Dorothy Moore, a husband and wife team of educational researchers whose independent research was showing surprising results—that formal instruction in math and reading was best put off until after age eight (Gaither, 2008, p. 130). The Moores began consulting with homeschooling families and they wrote several bestselling books including *Better Late Than Early* and *School Can Wait* (Gaither, 2008, p. 131).

Over time, the Moores became regular contributors to Holt's Growing Without Schooling newsletter, and after Raymond Moore appeared a number of times in the late 1970's on Dr. James Dobson's national Christian radio program, the concept of homeschooling came out of the homesteads and communes, and found its way into the world of Evangelical Christians and the Conservative Right (Gaither, 2008, p. 132).

In the 1980's, as many private Christian schools had to close their doors due to changes in tax status, a large number of Fundamentalist Christians who had already opted out of the "too Liberal" public schools (Isenberg, 2007, p. 388) found themselves scrambling to find an acceptable educational option for their children that would not involve sending them to the local secular public schools (Gaither, 2008, p. 111). Many Christian textbook publishers began marketing their educational products to this growing group of disenfranchised parents, and the "school-at-home" form of homeschooling was born. These parents attempted to reproduce in their homes the classroom settings of their children's former private schools.

As the academic success of homeschooling became apparent to the general public, the homeschooling movement shifted from being strictly the realm of two extremes—the Liberal Left and the Conservative Right—and into the mainstream (Wilhelm & Firmin, 2009, p. 310). Many public school districts around the country began to offer home-based, teacher-supervised learning options through both in-person and online venues as well as satellite, umbrella, charter, and correspondence programs through both public and private schools (Isenberg, 2007, p. 392).

Most of the recent homeschoolers joining the ranks appear to be motivated primarily by academic reasons. Ideological and religious reasons—although still strong—seem to be a less popular parental motivation for homeschooling than in years past (Collom, 2005, p. 331).

Parental Motivations for Homeschooling

Parents who choose to home educate their children are a diverse group and come from a wide range of ideological, academic, and pedagogical views (Collom, 2005, p. 331). To simplify things, Jane Van Galen looked at the most common reasons parents she interviewed chose to homeschool their children, and then categorized those reasons into two main categories she labeled ideology and pedagogy (1991, p. 66). The idea of two distinctly motivated types of homeschoolers—the Ideologues (religiously motivated) and the Pedagogues (academic and methodology motivated)—is a recurring theme throughout the available literature.

The Pedagogues are the philosophical offspring of John Holt and the early Liberal Left pioneers of the modern homeschooling movement. Pedagogues are concerned mainly with educational methods, improved learning environments for their children, and greater parental autonomy (Collom, 2005, p. 309-310). Many Pedagogues are either professional educators, themselves, or have done research and reading on their own about child development and educational methods (Van Galen, 1991, p. 71). Luke (2003) states, "these parents have deeply-held beliefs about learning, beliefs about which they feel strongly enough to practice at home with their children" (para. 9). The Pedagogues' "curriculum" usually consists of capitalizing on their children's natural curiosity and creativity, pursuing child-led interests, and making use of resources within the community (Van Galen, 1991, p. 73). Pedagogues are also more likely to be politically liberal and to practice more experimental styles of learning (Collom, 2005, p. 330).

The Ideologues are largely—but not exclusively— politically conservative Christian families who, as Raymond and Dorothy Moore observed, are "seeking to impart religious values to their children" (as cited in Collom, 2005, p. 309). Cai, Reeves and Robinson (2002) explain that these ideologically motivated parents desire to pass onto their children a set of beliefs, values, morals, and worldview which they believe to be absent in the secular public school system (p. 378). According to Van Galen (1991), the Ideologues tend to structure their homeschooling around a standard curriculum of textbooks and workbooks (p. 73), essentially recreating the traditional classroom setting in their homes. The Ideologues are also more likely to take standardized testing and the ensuing results more seriously than the Pedagogues (Collom, 2005, p. 330).

Collom (2005) suggests that as homeschooling has become more mainstream and less polarized between the two extremes, there are now actually four identifiable divisions in the reasons parents choose to homeschool their children: (1) Ideological, (2) pedagogical, (3) general dissatisfaction with the public schools, and (4) family-related reasons such as health concerns or special needs of their children (p. 311).

The ideological divide between the Liberal Left and the Conservative Right—between the secularly motivated and the religiously motivated—remains an on-going source of contention within the homeschooling community, itself (Isenberg, 2007, p. 388). Interestingly, Gaither (2008) observed that "to this day, many accounts of homeschooling written by [conservative Christian homeschoolers] do not even mention Holt or the entire left wing of the movement" (p. 144).

Discussion and Evaluation of Motivations

Van Galen (1991) did a service to future researchers when she simplified the reasons parents chose to homeschool into two categories: Ideologues and Pedagogues (p. 66). A previously difficult topic to fully understand became easier to describe and quantify. Although Van Galen's two categories are still in existence today, it would be naïve for a researcher to assume that all homeschoolers can easily be labeled as one or the other of these two groups now. Not only are some Christian parents homeschooling for pedagogical reasons—and "unschooling" parents homeschooling for religious reasons—but with the entry of the homeschooling movement into the mainstream of society, there are now more reasons than ever why parents choose this path for their families.

As Collom (2005) observed, most of homeschooling's recent converts are choosing to homeschool mainly for academic and family reasons with much less emphasis on the ideological and religious motivations (p. 331). The future of homeschooling will likely become less polarized as new people join the ranks, and perhaps may even swing back toward its more pedagogical roots.

Outcomes of Homeschooling

Homeschooling has consistently proven to be an academically valid educational option. In 1990, Dr. Brian Ray (2000) conducted a survey of 1,500 homeschooling families representing 4,600 homeschooled children, the largest study of its kind at the time. Ray observed that "the home-educated students averaged at or above the 80th percentile on standardized achievement tests in all subject areas," while the average public school result was the 50th percentile (p. 74).

According to a 1999 research study conducted by L. M. Rudner which measured the academic achievement of 20,000+ homeschooled students, standardized test scores for homeschoolers fell consistently between the 75th and 85th percentiles (as cited in Wilhelm & Firmin, 2009, p. 310). Other studies have had similar findings (Ray, 2000, p. 74-75).

Ray (2000) stated that some correlations were noted between the parents' education and income levels, but even with these correlations, homeschooled students with parents of lower education and income levels still scored higher on standardized tests than their public schooled counterparts with the same parental variables (p. 76). The most significant variables in Ray's (2000) study were the parents' educational level (which affected the student's total language scores), the number of years the student was taught at home (also affected total language scores), the gender of the student (girls generally outperformed boys on the standardized tests), and the frequency of visits to the public library (affected reading scores) (p. 88).

Collom (2005) found several factors that were statistically significant in the outcome of homeschooling: 1) The parents' political views, 2) the parents' level of education, and 3) the parents' dissatisfaction with the public school system (p. 331). Surprisingly, the children of politically conservative parents did better in math, while the children of liberal parents had stronger language skills (Collom, 2005, p. 326). Collom (2005) theorizes that this is probably related more to other variables such as teaching-style and attitudes toward standardized testing than being directly related to political ideology (p. 330). Parents who are homeschooling because of their dissatisfaction with the public schools tend to have students with some of the highest reading and language scores (Collom, 2005, p. 330).

According to Ray (2000), in conventional school classrooms a number of variables have consistently proven to increase academic achievement in the students. Many of these factors are naturally part of the homeschooling life: One-on-one tutoring, increased teacher feedback to the student, direct instruction by the teacher, increased academic engaged time, mastery learning, cooperative learning, increased contextualization of teaching in experiences in the home and community, and increased involvement of parents (p. 91-92). Ray theorizes that if these factors are inherently a part of the homeschooling environment, and it appears that they are, "then it may be likely they would work to the advantage of home school students" (Ray, 2000, p. 92).

Cai et al. (2002) observed that because of the close relationship between the teacher/parent and the student/child, the homeschooling teacher can easily individualize daily instruction to the specific needs of each child (p. 373), essentially creating in their homes the most ideal learning environment available, one-on-one tutoring (Ray, 2000, p. 91).

More Discussion and Evaluation of Outcomes

If parents choose to homeschool because they are looking for increased academic achievement as measured by standardized achievement tests, the research shows that any method of homeschooling will most likely raise their child's test scores above those of their traditionally schooled counterparts (Ray, 2000, p. 74-75). But if parents are choosing to homeschool because they are looking beyond a simple test score and perhaps looking for outcomes in more subjective areas such as character and critical thinking, the question needs to be asked once again, are all homeschooling methods created equal?

Conclusion of Literature Review

The currently available scholarly research on homeschooling methods and outcomes is still somewhat limited at this point. It mainly focuses on the history of homeschooling, the motivations of homeschooling parents, and the standardized testing outcomes of the students. Questions still remain that will need to be answered directly from homeschoolers, themselves, and from homeschooling families' and experts' own literature, such as what methods are being used in actual homeschooling families, and what sort of results are these parents seeing in their children?

The main focus of the remainder of this article will be on which method—or methods—would most likely produce Gatto's desired educational outcomes, or is there perhaps a combination of methods that may work better than any single method? Further research into the main homeschooling methods used today, and how each fits with Gatto's thoughts in his essay, "Against School" will be explored in the next section.

Brief Descriptions of Popular Homeschooling Methods

Unschooling is based on many of the early teachings of John Holt. It is essentially student-directed learning without a scope-and-sequence plan, focusing on the interests of the child, and allowing the student to pursue their varied interests as far and wide as they personally choose. Classical education has a heavy focus on rote learning and basic facts in the early grades, with an increasing emphasis on critical thinking and oratory in the later years. The Charlotte Mason method is based on the teachings of a British educator from the late 19th and early 20th centuries who focused on children developing a lifetime love of learning. Correspondence and umbrella schools vary greatly depending upon the school they are affiliated with, but usually tend to rely heavily on workbooks, textbooks, and fill-in-the-blank quizzes and tests. Traditional "school-at-home" education attempts to re-create the schoolroom at home, sometimes to the point of school desks lined up in a row, morning flag salutes, and chalkboards, as well as relying on textbooks, workbooks, teacher-focused lectures, and traditional testing methods. Cooperative schooling is usually done by a group of like-minded homeschooling families with each parent in the group taking on a teaching role in one or more subjects of particular interest or expertise. Computer-based home education can be purchased as a stand-alone curriculum, or as part of a correspondence program with a wide range of methodologies available (Levison, personal communication, April 2010; Ray, 2000, December).

Gatto's Description of the Educated State

Rather than children simply passing—or even excelling at—standardized tests, or just meeting compulsory attendance criteria, Gatto would prefer the outcome of education to be along the lines of personal maturity, independence, creativity, and critical thinking. While these subjective goals are more difficult to measure than straight-forward test results in

Math or Reading, Gatto's thirty years of working professionally in the trenches of New York's public schools have made him a well-respected and acknowledged expert in both scholarly and homeschooling circles on the methods necessary to reach the outcomes he is looking to see in successfully educated students.

Using Gatto's suggestions from his article, "Against School," and his book, *A Different Kind of Teacher*, as an outline for achieving Gatto's definition of educational success, several common homeschooling methods will be examined and critiqued with the result showing that a combination of Charlotte Mason's methods and unschooling would most likely best represent the means to achieve Gatto's goals for parent teachers with their homeschooled students.

According to Gatto (2001), the process of "education describes efforts largely self-initiated for the purpose of taking charge of your life wisely and living in a world you understand. The educated state is a complex tapestry woven out of broad experience, grueling commitments, and substantial risk" (p. 49). This highly subjective description of what it means to be an educated person is explained in further detail throughout Gatto's writings, especially as outlined in the pages of his book, *A Different Kind of Teacher: Solving the Crisis of American Schooling*, and his Harper's essay, "Against School" (Gatto, 2003). His combined "curriculum" as stated in the preceding sources, can be condensed into the following general description of methods Gatto recommends to achieve a well-rounded education:

Teach serious material

- History
- Literature (real books)
- Philosophy
- Music
- Art
- Economics
- Theology
- Be flexible about time, textbooks, materials, and tests

Encourage maturity

- Think critically and independently
- Self-control
- Financial responsibility
- Self-entertainment
- Capacity for insight
- Examine political and commercial statements
- Develop deep friendships/relationships

Train to be leaders and adventurers

- Encourage curiosity and questions
- Give autonomy to take risks now and then
- Adventure
- Resilience
- Introduce kids to competent adults

The Charlotte Mason Method and Unschooling

When researching the various homeschooling methods most frequently used today, the one that stood out as being the most academically similar to what Gatto describes (the teaching of serious material) was the Charlotte Mason method. According to Levison (2000), Mason developed a lifetime love of learning in her students by engaging the children firsthand with nature, literature, science, history, art, music, and avoiding dumbed-down materials as much as possible. The main focus of Mason's educational ideas and philosophy was having the students read top quality literature—real books rather than textbooks— and delving into a wide variety of serious topics throughout childhood (p. 7-9). Mason described most literature written to children as "twaddle" and felt that childish materials should be avoided at all costs.

Gatto stated that "I always knew real books and schoolbooks were different," and he felt he had found proof of that when reading a school edition of Moby Dick—essentially a package of prefabricated, prethought questions and ideas, what he considered "a disguised indoctrination" rather than a real book (p. 69). Charlotte Mason would most likely have agreed with Gatto's critique of modern schoolbooks and texts.

Another of Mason's methods that fits with Gatto's desired curriculum is the process of narration. Narration is essentially the "telling back" of material learned. It focuses the child's mind on what they have been reading or studying, and they then need to pick and choose what to narrate and what to leave unsaid. In the book *When Children Love to Learn*, Maryellen St. Cyr states that when "practiced with the right books, narration would provide the food upon which the mind could grow and thrive" (Beckman, J., St. Cyr, M., Scott, B., and Macaulay, S. S., 2004, p. 128). Levison (2000) describes this process as oral essay writing and according to Levison, Mason says that narration "is not a mere act of memory because we let their minds act on the material in their own original way. They will classify and connect information" as they see fit (p. 11-14). This sounds like an introduction to Gatto's desired critical thinking because it definitely is not just a parroting back of rote facts and memorized information, but requires the children to make connections within themselves.

Charlotte Mason recommended that parents involved with her PNEU (Parents National Education Union) correspondence schools should finish teaching all academic subjects in the morning hours before noon, leaving the afternoons and evenings free each day for the children to pursue handiwork, crafts, outdoor play, and self-entertainment (Levison, 2000, p. 53). This idea is definitely in keeping with Gatto's description of encouraging maturity, leadership, and adventure.

Because of the strong emphasis in the Charlotte Mason method on serious adult-level material—avoiding twaddle—this method would ensure the academic and educational goals Gatto outlines, while also providing time in the afternoons for self-regulated blocks of time each day for the students to develop their own interests and adventures. By adding in the following concepts of unschooling during the students free-time, the full Gatto curriculum could be achieved easily in the homeschooling family.

Unschooling is essentially providing an education through the natural connections and activities in the child's world, following their interests and aptitudes, without teaching within the confines of the rigid structures of conventional schooling, but as Gatto stated, "Unschooled, perhaps, but not uneducated" (2003). John Holt, in his bestselling book *How Children*

Learn, best describes what unschooling looks like in the life of a child: "What we need to do, and all we need to do, is bring as much of the world as we can into the school and classroom (in our case, into their lives); give children as much help and guidance as they ask for; listen respectfully when they feel like talking; and then get out of the way. We can trust them to do the rest" (Holt, 1995).

Unschooling provides the student with nearly unlimited opportunities for adventure, self-entertainment, and autonomy, and by engaging children actively in the world around them, they have the chance to learn directly from competent adults in the community and to engage with adult-level topics of all sorts.

An interesting side note is that the Charlotte Mason method found its way into modern homeschooling through the Conservative Christian wing of homeschooling (the Idealogues), while unschooling developed in the Liberal Left (the Pedagogues). By combining both of these popular homeschooling methods in their educational efforts, parents today can benefit from homeschooling pioneers in both realms of today's home education movement.

Other Homeschooling Methods

In "Against School," Gatto had a number of strong complaints against the public schools and the regular forms of compulsory education. His main concerns were the high level of boredom in schools—of both the students and the teachers—and also the childishness that was encouraged by not allowing the students to develop their full leadership skills, intellectual capabilities, and inner thought life. Simply recreating the standard classroom setting in the home would not necessarily produce the results Gatto would like to see in children.

As stated earlier, research shows that any method of homeschooling will raise children's test scores above those of their traditionally schooled counterparts (Ray, 2000, p. 74-75), but if the parents' goal is more subjective in nature, their choice of homeschooling methods needs to be carefully thought out.

If a parent chose another popular form of home education—Classical education, unit studies, traditional school-at-home, correspondence schools and school-related umbrella organizations, cooperatives, and computer-based options—they would still most likely see positive results academically in their homeschooled students but not necessarily the subjective results or processes Gatto recommends. For example, Classical education, with its heavy emphasis on rote learning in the early grades, would have the possibility of developing into boredom for both the student and teacher; something Gatto wants parents and teachers to avoid in the educational process. Unit studies have the potential to be anything the teacher designs, so by keeping in mind Gatto's educational goals and "curriculum," that method could be easily adapted with aspects of Charlotte Mason and unschooling added in. Traditional school-at-home education, cooperative classrooms, computer curriculum, and school-related umbrella programs all have the potential to create the very same environment for homeschoolers that Gatto was concerned about in the public schools.

Much of what Gatto describes as being missing from the public schools can be provided easily in the homeschool, no matter which educational method a parent chooses, simply by making a few modifications and using techniques from unschooling and the Charlotte Mason method in combination with whatever curriculum or method they have chosen for their family. For example, by applying Charlotte Mason's ideas about finishing academics in the morning hours and then leaving the afternoon free for exploration and "unschooling," any homeschooling method could produce more of Gatto's results of building maturity, leadership, and adventure into children's lives.

If a parent were using a more traditional textbook approach to home education, they could supplement textbook reading with real books on the same topics. For example, if a textbook or a literature anthology included a snippet from Dickens' *Oliver Twist*, the parent could assign the entire book as required reading so the child would benefit from and interact with the full message the author originally intended rather than just a small segment of the book presented out-of-context and with discussion questions already provided by the textbook editor.

Conclusion

To answer the question initially raised in this article—are all homeschooling methods created equal?—the answer is no. Although all methods of homeschooling can produce standardized test results that put the public schools to shame, not all methods will produce the same level of personal maturity, leadership, and intellectual capabilities in the students. For the conscientious parent looking to see their children develop into the self-reliant, critical thinkers Gatto described in the "Against School" essay and his other works, a combination of Charlotte Mason's methods and unschooling would have the best chance of success. For the interested parent looking to homeschool their children with these methods, or even to supplement their child's public school experience with some of these proven homeschooling techniques, numerous books, articles, and websites are available that detail the practical how-to's of both unschooling and the Charlotte Mason method.

References

Beckman, J., St Cyr, M., Scott, B., & Macaulay, S. S. (2004). *When children love to learn: A practical application of Charlotte Mason's philosophy for today* (E. Cooper, Ed.). Wheaton, Illinois: Crossway Books.

Cai, Y., Reeve, J., & Robinson, D. T. (2002). Home schooling and teaching style: Comparing the motivating styles of home school and public school teachers. Journal of Educational Psychology, 94(2), 372-380.

Collom, E. (2005, January). The ins and outs of homeschooling; the detriments of parental motivations and student acheivement. Education and Urban Society, 37(3), 307-335.

Dobson, L. (2000). *Homeschoolers' success stories: 15 adults and 12 young people share the impact that homeschooling has made on their lives.* New York: Prima Publishing.

Gaither, M. (2008). *Homeschool: An American history.* New York: Palgrave Macmillan.

Gatto, J. T. (2000). *The underground history of American*

education: A school teacher's intimate investigation into the problem of modern schooling. New York: Oxford Village Press.

Gatto, J. T. (2001). *A different kind of teacher: Solving the crisis of American schooling.* Berkeley, CA: Berkeley Hills Books.

Gatto, J. T. (2003, September). Against school: How public education cripples our kids, and why [Article from Harper's].

Holt, J. (1995). *How children learn* (Revised ed.). Cambridge, Massachusetts: Da Capo Press. (Original work published 1967)

Isenberg, E. J. (2007). What have we learned about homeschooling? Peabody Journal of Edcuation, 82(2-3), 387-409.

Levison, C. (2000). *A Charlotte Mason education: A home schooling how-to manual.* Beverly Hills, California: Champion Press, Ltd.

Luke, C. (2003, April 3). Homeschooling: Learning from dissent. Canadian Journal of Educational Administration and Policy, 25.

Macleod, D. I. (2009, June). Homeschool: An American history [Review of the book Homeschool: An American history]. The Journal of American History, 96(1), 179.

Mencken, H. L. (1924). The goslings: A study of the American schools. In RALPH: The review of arts, literature, philosophy and the humanities (par. 7) [Book Review].

National Center for Education Statistics. (2008, December). 1.5 million homeschooled students in the United States in 2007. In Issue Brief [Fact sheet from U.S. Department of Education].

Ray, B. D., Ph.D. (2000). Home schooling: The ameliorator of negative influences in learning? Peabody Journal of Education, 75(1&2), 71-106.

Ray, B. D., Ph.D. (2000, December). Homeschooling teaching strategies [Article]. Retrieved from ERIC (Educational Resources Information Center) database.

Ray, B. D., Ph.D. (2004). *Home educated and now adults: Their community and civic involvement, views about homeschooling, and other traits.* Salem, OR: NEHRI Publications.

Taylor, D. (2009, January 2). John Taylor Gatto: On life and education [Video file].

Van Galen, J. A. (1991). Ideologues and pedagogues: Parents who teach their children at home. In J. Van Galen (Ed.), Social and Policy Issues in Education: The University of Cincinnati Series: *Home schooling: Political, historical, and pedagogical perspectives* (pp. 63-76). Norwood, New Jersey: Ablex Publishing Corporation.

Wilhelm, G. M., & Firmin, M. W. (2009). Historical and contemporary developments in home school education. Journal of Research on Christian Education, 18, 303-315.

ABOUT THE AUTHOR

Deborah Taylor-Hough is a graduate of the University of Washington with an interdisciplinary Literature degree (*magna cum laude*) and is currently a Graduate student pursuing a Master of Fine Arts in Creative Writing and Poetics. After finishing Grad school, she hopes to teach at a local community college or university, and also start a writing and educational resource center for homeschoolers (and others) based on Charlotte Mason methods and principles.

Deborah is also the author of a number of traditionally published books including the bestselling *Frozen Assets* cookbook series (SourceBooks) and the popular *Frugal Living for Dummies*® (Wiley). Deborah has worked as a newspaper columnist, radio host, church outreach director, and helped run an antique mall. But her all-time favorite job/vocation has been being Mom to her three (now adult) kiddos.

Deborah began researching home education 30+ years ago, several years before her oldest child's birth. She successfully home educated her children all the way through high school using a relaxed version of Charlotte Mason's methods mixed with afternoons of unschooling.

The final ten years of Deborah's homeschooling adventures were completed as essentially a single mom after her husband was diagnosed with a degenerative brain disorder and needed to move out of their home for safety reasons.

Deborah has had websites and blogs about Charlotte Mason homeschooling for many years and teaches workshops at churches, women's groups, and homeschooling conferences on Charlotte Mason homeschooling topics, frugal living, cooking for the freezer, homemaking, and parenting. She was the editor of The Charlotte Mason Monthly newsletter, and has facilitated homeschooling groups of various types (4H, nature study, journalism, literature, etc.). Deborah is available to conduct in-person Twaddle-Free Education™ workshops, and for one-on-one homeschooling consultations (in-person, or via phone or email).

Deborah is in the process of publishing the "Charlotte Mason Topics" book series. Each book is a compilation of Charlotte Mason's writings from her original six-volume set on various topics including the formation of habits, nature study, geography, history, language arts, and more

Visit Deborah online at:

CharlotteMasonHome.com
TheSimpleMom.com
FrozenAssets.info

ABOUT "CHARLOTTE MASON TOPICS"

The first two volumes from the new "Charlotte Mason Topics" series are now available. Several more topical volumes are currently in the works and will be released during Spring and Summer 2015.

Habits: The Mother's Secret of Success
(Charlotte Mason Topics, Volume 1)

Book Number One in the "Charlotte Mason Topics" series is a compilation of Mason's teachings on the formation of habits. Mason's ideas on the formation of habit are a key to understanding how to make lasting change in a child, or even yourself.

Contents include:

- Habit May Supplant "Nature"
- The Formation of Habit
- Childhood and Nursery Habits
- The Habit of Attention
- The Habit of Obedience
- Habits of Truth and Temper
- … and more

The Outdoor Life of Children:
The Importance of Nature Study and Outside Activities
(Charlotte Mason Topics, Volume 2)

The Outdoor Life of Children is Book Number Two from the new "Charlotte Mason Topics" series Mason had a strong emphasis on the importance of children being out-of-doors, both for Nature Study, and also for their healthy physical and mental growth and development.

Contents include:

- Knowledge Through Senses
- Out-of-Door Geography
- Flowers and Trees
- 'Living Creatures'
- Field-Lore and Naturalists' Books
- Walks in Bad Weather
- Teaching Natural Philosophy
- … and more

Other Titles by Deborah Taylor-Hough

Frugal Living for Dummies® (Wiley)

Frozen Assets: Cook for a Day, Eat for a Month (SourceBooks)

Frozen Assets Lite & Easy (SourceBooks)

A Simple Choice: A Practical Guide for Saving Your Time, Money & Sanity (Simple Pleasures Press)

Mix-and-Match Recipes: Creative Ideas for Today's Busy Kitchens (Simple Pleasures Press)

Frozen Assets Readers' Favorites (Simple Pleasures Press)

Basics of Inductive Bible Study (Lulu.com)

For details: thesimplemom.com/welcome/my-books/

CPSIA information can be obtained at www.ICGtesting.com
Printed in the USA
LVOW07s0505271115

464318LV00015B/560/P

9 780692 431283